SOUVENIR POST CARDS

from

ORKNEY

Orkney in Picture Postcards

Compiled by
NORMAN HUDSON

D1277144

The Shetland Times Ltd.
Lerwick
1994

First published 1994

ISBN 1 898852 00 6

Introduction and compilation © Norman Hudson

British Library Cataloguing-in-Publication Data

A catalogue record for this book is available from the
British Library.

Printed and published by
The Shetland Times Ltd.,
Prince Alfred Street, Lerwick, Shetland,
Scotland.

CONTENTS

The "Golden Age" of picture postcards in Britain occurred between about 1902 and the First World War. Postcard fever swept the nation and almost every household owned at least one album. Their geographic remoteness did not prevent Orcadians sharing the nationwide craze. "Another p.c. for your collection", is a message often found on postcards from this time. When the British later flooded to the seaside in their millions, the vagaries of the British climate then became the main and inescapable topic on many a picture postcard!

Almost every aspect of life came to be depicted on picture postcards. Whether the collector's own interests lay in local views, music-hall stars, cats or flowers, the postcard publishers catered for all tastes and, of course, endeavoured to stimulate new demands for their products. In the days before large-scale tourism and long before the arrival of television documentaries, picture postcards of Orkney, for instance, could show a way of life significantly different to the everyday experiences of friends and relatives living on mainland Britain.

The cards posted and collected in the Edwardian era were, however, quite different from the very first postcards, which had been produced over 30 years earlier. The world's first postcard is generally recognised as that issued by the Imperial Austrian postal service in October 1869. These "Correspondenz-Karte" were plain and rather smaller than the postcards we associate with Edwardian times but, largely because they could be posted at half the cost of posting a letter, they were instantly popular with the public. Other countries followed the Austrian example, the first British postcard being issued by the General Post Office just one year later.

The first picture postcards appeared in France in the early 1870s. Picture postcard production then gathered momentum throughout the 1880s and 1890s, largely through advances in printing techniques in Germany. On 1st September, 1894, Britain's Post Office finally permitted private firms to print and issue picture postcards. At the Post Office's insistence, the back of the card was reserved solely for the recipient's address, and so the illustration – often little more than small engravings or line drawings covering only a section of the postcard's front – had to share the front with a necessarily brief written message. These cards are known, logically, as "undivided backs", and it was not until January 1902 that the Post Office finally allowed the back to be divided in two – with the left side for the sender's message and the right for the address – freeing the whole of the front for the illustration.

German influence in postcard printing remained very strong throughout these early years, with many British-published cards, including those with views of Orkney, being printed in, say, Berlin or Saxony. This ended when the Great War suddenly made the "Printed in Germany" inscription a hindrance to the postcard's sale.

The First World War largely brought an end to the "Golden Age" of picture postcard collecting. The precise cause of this is still a matter of debate. Increasing cinema-going and the ownership of personal cameras were probably contributory. Postcards continued to be published, of course, but the era of mass collecting had come to an end. The legacies of this age now find the light of day from time to time often when attics are sorted. These postcards – some (the commonest) changing hands for just a few pence, and others (the rarest) worth many pounds – are now sought after because they can provide a unique pictorial record of a moment in time frozen forever by the camera and of a way of life long gone.

INTRODUCTION
ORKNEY IN PICTURE POSTCARDS

Orkney's way of life and the islands' history and traditions have been well depicted ever since the earliest days of picture postcards. In the early years, for example, George Washington Wilson & Co. of Aberdeen produced postcards showing views of Orkney largely photographed by Wilson himself (1823-1893) during his visits to the islands in the 1880s and early 1890s. This continued until the company went into liquidation in 1908. Many of Wilson's photographs are now preserved by the University of Aberdeen. In addition, a number of nationally-renowned publishers – notably James Valentine & Sons of Dundee — featured Orcadian views in their sales catalogues over the years.

In many ways, however, it is the postcards produced by Orkney's own local photographers – sometimes in quite limited quantities – which often provide the greatest interest today. In this respect, Orkney has been blessed – from the earliest days right up to the present – with photographers having an eye capable of capturing local views and lifestyles for picture postcard production. Several names will feature prominently in this volume.

It will be noted that postcards produced by Tom Kent feature heavily in this volume, far more than any other photographer. His personal contribution to Orkney's photographic archive is unparalleled.

Over the years he produced a prolific number of picture postcards from his own photographs. These postcards are eminently collectable. Many of his real-photographic cards, in particular, are much sought-after by collectors and can be found with high price-labels in postcard dealers' stocks.

Tom Kent was born in the parish of Firth in 1863. As a young man he emigrated to the USA where he worked in a Chicago drug store. It was here that he developed his enduring passion for photography. Returning to Orkney in 1897, he opened a professional photographer's shop in Albert Street, Kirkwall, in the following year. Soon afterwards he moved to larger premises at 7 Broad Street from which he sold photographic equipment, stationery, fancy goods and, of course, postcards. Using some of the most sophisticated equipment available at the time, Tom Kent produced an enormous variety of photographs, recording life in Orkney over the next thirty years. He had an artist's eye for composition and many of his photographs are rightly regarded as works of art. Sadly, by the time of his death on 11th August, 1936, Tom Kent had obviously fallen on hard times since his death passed almost unnoticed by the society he had recorded so superbly. More happily, a large number of his original glass plates, together with some of his photographic equipment, are now in the care of the Orkney Museum service. A major exhibition of his work was staged at the Pier Arts Centre, Stromness, in 1989.

Also prominent amongst the names of local postcard producers is that of William Hourston. Willie Hourston had been born in Evie in 1895 and moved to Stromness in the 1930s. For a time he ran a billiard saloon and barber's shop but, as time passed, photography took up more and more of his time. His photographic output – with many of his photographs being published as picture postcards – was primarily concentrated in the Stromness area. Many of his postcard views are truly stunning. Willie Hourston continued to take photographs until his retirement in the late 1950s. He continued to live in Stromness until his death in 1968.

No mention of local postcard-producers would be complete without reference to The Leonards, a stationer's shop in Kirkwall. The shop produced its own range of picture postcards in the early years of the twentieth century and, happily, continues to sell postcards from its premises at 1 Albert Street to the present day.

The work of several other Orcadian photographers and postcard-producers, not specifically mentioned in this brief introduction, is included in this volume. We are grateful to them, one and all, since, collectively, they have left us with a detailed record of life in Orkney over the last hundred years. This is a precious photographic legacy which most other parts of the British Isles cannot match.

THE AUTHOR

"SOUVENIR POSTCARDS FROM ORKNEY"

Like many visitors to Orkney, I fell under the islands' spell on my very first visit. Soon afterwards I started to collect postmarks and picture postcards not only as an armchair way of visiting the islands but also because I soon realised that the postcards themselves contained a vital pictorial record of a unique Orkney history slipping even further into the past

It is no coincidence that the work of Tom Kent features heavily in this volume. Ever since I added the first of his real-photographic postcards to my collection, I have sought out his work with considerable eagerness. Each new Tom Kent postcard brings a great sense of joy.

In this book I have endeavoured to bring together a selection of postcards to show a wide cross-section of Orkney's history, landscape and lifestyle. In preparing the accompanying text I have tried to be informative without being too heavyweight. After all, this is not intended to be a volume of local history. A number of publications by authors far better equipped to perform such a task are already available. I would certainly wish to express my thanks to Bryce Wilson, Orkney Islands Council's Museums Officer (at Kirkwall's excellent Tankerness House Museum) who provided useful information about several postcards before this book became a possibility and who so kindly gave of his time and knowledge in checking my text and making several useful suggestions for amendments.

The postcards selected are all from my own collection and, taken together, are intended to give a pictorial history of the islands of Orkney, a small part of the world treasured by many. In the future I intend to donate my collection of Orkney postcards and postal history to Tankerness House Museum in the hope that it might give the pleasure to others which it continues to give to me. In the meantime, I dedicate this volume to Jim Horsford, with whom I shared my first rewarding visit to Orkney and with whom I have since journeyed many a memorable mile.

Norman Hudson, 1994

Norman Hudson

Norman Hudson was born near Wellington, Shropshire, in 1953. After graduating in 1974 with a BA degree in geography and history, Mr Hudson took up a local government administrative post with a district council near Chester where he has lived and worked every since.

His love of travel led to many holidays visiting the islands of Scotland. Orkney and Shetland soon became his favourite destinations, and several holidays visiting the islands led to the start of a collection of postcards and postmarks from both Orkney and Shetland which now numbers several thousand items.

His first book, "Souvenir Postcards from Shetland: Shetland in Picture Postcards", was published by The Shetland Times Limited in 1992.

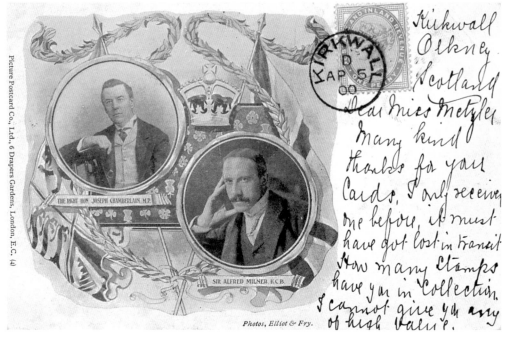

Early picture postcard from Orkney (not with an Orcadian subject) bearing a Victorian halfpenny stamp and sent to a fellow postcard collector in the Netherlands.

Orkney's reliance on shipping for links with the outside world is as old as the islands'
first habitation. Yet it was to be well into the nineteenth century before regular shipping
links to mainland Scotland were to be introduced. The Aberdeen, Leith, Clyde and Tay
Shipping Company began the first scheduled commercial steamer service in 1833, operating
between Aberdeen, Leith, Wick and Kirkwall. The much shorter route – across the Pentland
Firth – was boosted in 1874 when the Highland Railway completed its line to Thurso.

Published by John Rae, Stationer, Stromness

Scapa Pier – Departure of Mailboat „St.Ola."

1. "SCAPA PIER – DEPARTURE OF MAILBOAT 'ST OLA' "
For many years, the ferry service from Scrabster (near Thurso) to Stromness (which had begun in
1856) operated via Scapa Pier, the nearest point on Scapa Flow to Kirkwall (just two miles north of
the pictured location). Mails to and from all parts of Orkney under Kirkwall's control would be loaded
and unloaded here. This intermediate call was discontinued after the Second World War, enabling
the ferry to take the shorter, direct route to Stromness via the west side of the island of Hoy.

3194.   S.S. ST. OLA AT STROMNESS.

2. "S.S. ST OLA AT STROMNESS"
The 231 ton *St Ola* entered the service of the North of Scotland and Orkney & Shetland Steam
Navigation Company (known as "the North Company" for short) in 1892, operating the company's
Scrabster-Stromness route. She was to become one of the great veterans of British shipping,
providing one of Orkney's vital shipping links with the Scottish mainland through two world
wars until her retirement in 1951, a faithful service lasting 59 years.

The North Company's ships became household names in Orkney and their comings and goings were the subject of everyday conversations. The company itself was taken over by Coast Lines in 1961 and subsequently became part of the P&O group. P&O celebrated the 150th anniversary of the Orkney and Shetland shipping services in 1987 and, fittingly, produced souvenir postcards showing the company's vessels, past and present.

3. "THE ROAD TO THURSO"

The 750 ton motor vessel *St Ola* was the second ship of that name to be operated by the North Company. She provided the Stromness-Scrabster service from 1951 until 1974. On its southbound journey in this view, the *St Ola* is seen against the background of Hoy. Ward Hill (at 1,571', the highest point in Orkney) and St John's Head (one of the highest and most dramatic sea-cliffs in Britain) dominate the landscape. P&O's current ferry on the Scrabster-Stromness service is the fourth ship to bear the name "St Ola". She took over the service in 1992.

4. "S.S. ST MAGNUS AT KIRKWALL"

When built in 1924, the 1,591 ton *St Magnus* (the third ship of that name) was by far the largest ship yet built for the North Company. She provided the company's weekend service between 1924 and 1939 and earned a reputation as being a good sea-boat. She was requisitioned by the Admiralty during 1939 and 1940 and took part in the Norwegian campaign. She continued to serve Orkney and Shetland after the war until finally sold for breaking up in 1960.

Methods of transportation within and between the islands of Orkney have advanced beyond
all recognition in the twentieth century. Road transport has kept pace with developments elsewhere
but, in terms of air transport, Orcadians were to become the most air-minded people in Britain.
In 1933, Highland Airways started a regular Inverness-Kirkwall service and Britain's
first regular internal airmail service commenced on this route on 29th May, 1934.

5. "ORKNEY MOTOR EXPRESS"

E. J. Robertson Grant established the Orkney Express coach and car services, based in Junction
Road, Kirkwall. Mr Grant himself is seen driving the Sterling bus along the Kirkwall-Stromness road in
this 1905 photograph by Tom Kent, printed as a postcard in "Kent's Orcadian Series" and posted at
Kirkwall on 24th July, 1905. The array of fine hats suggests that this was a special excursion.

6. "U.S. WORLD FLIERS, HOUTON BAY 30.7.24"

A group of six American aviators in three Douglas bi-planes (named "Chicago", "Boston" and
"New Orleans") arrived in Orkney on 30th July, 1924, on their 18,000 mile round-the-world flight.
The group's leader was Lieutenant Lowell H. Smith. They had set off from Santa Monica, California,
on 17th March and had arrived in Orkney from Brough, near Hull (a distance of 370 miles),
before setting out for Torshavn, Faroe Islands (275 miles) on the next leg of their epic
flight. They hoped to return to California by 1st September. On a less epic scale, Loganair
was to commence its invaluable inter-island services in Orkney in 1967.

Orkney's main island is simply called "the Mainland" but is sometimes shown as "Pomona" or even "Hrossey" (its old Norse name) on older maps. Orkney's only towns, Kirkwall and Stromness, are both situated on the Mainland. Whilst Stromness was still a small village at the beginning of the eighteenth century, Kirkwall has long been a place of some importance. Kirkwall is the largest town and is the administrative and commercial capital of the islands.

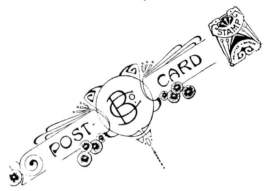

I'm having a champion time at Kirkwall

What's more! I aint coming home till I'm forced.

7. "I'M HAVING A CHAMPION TIME AT KIRKWALL"

Postcard publishers – in this case, Bamforth & Co. of Holmfirth, Yorkshire – featured many general comic postcards in their catalogues which could be overprinted with the name of any town or resort. While the image of a bucket and spade and the background of white cliffs might not immediately reflect the Orkney landscape, an enterprising local shopkeeper was obviously attracted by the idea.

Don't Grouse.

Come to KIRKWALL.

8. "DON'T GROUSE. COME TO KIRKWALL"

A flap on this anonymously-published "novelty card" lifts up to reveal a folded sequence of twelve photographs of Orkney scenes. It is quite common to find such postcards bearing "postage due" labels as most writers were unaware that the Post Office insisted that the usual halfpenny postcard rate would increase to a penny if the sender wrote more than "five words of a complimentary character".

The name "Kirkwall" is a corruption of the Norse "Kirkjuvagr", meaning "church bay", suggesting that a Celtic christian settlement existed at this location when Viking raiders and settlers arrived in the ninth century. Kirkwall remained a small village until the twelfth century when the construction of St Magnus' Cathedral provided a spur to development.

St. Magnus Cathedral

Kirkwall

From St. Magnus Tower

9. "KIRKWALL"

Sent from Kirkwall to Yorkshire in May 1910, this WR&S "Reliable Series" postcard shows St Magnus Cathedral together with a view of Kirkwall's roofscape from the Cathedral tower. In many ways the Cathedral is the heart and soul of Kirkwall. The postcard also depicts the badge of the Royal Burgh of Kirkwall together with its motto, "Si Deus Nobiscum" ("If God is with us").

10. "KIRKWALL FROM WEST"

Tom Kent's postcard shows what is – or was – the view of Kirkwall when arriving from the direction of Stromness. This view of the town, dominated by St Magnus Cathedral, is across the inland body of water known as the Peerie Sea, separated from Kirkwall Bay by a narrow spit of land known as the Ayre. Ayre Road is built along its length. Land reclamation has greatly reduced the size of the Peerie Sea since this postcard was published.

KIRKWALL

Kirkwall grew steadily as a commercial and administrative centre following the founding of St Magnus Cathedral in 1137. The growth and success of the town was recognised when Kirkwall was granted Burgh status by Royal Charter in 1486. Kirkwall was to retain this distinctive status right up until 1975 when the all-purpose Orkney Islands Council was created.

T. Kent Publisher, Kirkwall

Kirkwall from Cathedral Tower

11. "KIRKWALL FROM CATHEDRAL TOWER"
This view of Kirkwall is seen when looking in a north-westerly direction from the Cathedral tower. The Peerie Sea can just be seen on the left. The large building to the upper right (facing the harbour) is the Kirkwall Hotel. Towards the bottom left, with its twin gables facing onto Castle Street, was the Castle Hotel (see postcard No.26).

12. "KIRKWALL FROM CATHEDRAL TOWER"
Tom Kent's postcard, with its panoramic view from the Cathedral tower, had earlier been published with the title "American Minesweepers in Bay". It shows a large visiting flotilla anchored in Kirkwall Bay.

Echoing trends in rural communities elsewhere, the population of Orkney as a whole has fallen from its peak of 32,225 in 1861 to about 21,300 today. At the same time, the population of Kirkwall itself has continued to increase. The town's population was about 3,500 in 1861 but today's urban area is home to about 6,700 people. This means that almost one third of Orkney's total population now lives in the islands' main town and that there are now far more people living in Kirkwall than in all the South and North Isles put together.

13. "KIRKWALL FROM DUNDAS CRESCENT"

As Kirkwall grew, its urban area spread eastwards and southwards. Dundas Crescent represents an early stage of the expansion to the east. It is a sweeping curve lined with stone villas built in the late nineteenth century. The panoramic view of Kirkwall on this postcard shows St Magnus Cathedral on the left. On the right is the East Church, a substantial place of worship, built in 1847.

14. "KIRKWALL"

This fine aerial view shows Kirkwall's piers and harbour and the town spreading out beyond in a southerly direction. Ships providing regular services between Aberdeen and Lerwick have included Kirkwall as a port of call since the mid-nineteenth century. In addition, the ships which link Kirkwall with Orkney's North Isles operate from the east pier. This regular service first began in 1865.

KIRKWALL
THE HARBOUR

In the early nineteenth century, goods and passengers arriving by sea at Kirkwall had to be transferred to small boats for ferrying ashore at the ayre, the narrow spit of land separating Kirkwall Bay from the Peerie Sea. The east pier – facing the end of Bridge Street – was completed in 1811 and the west pier was started two years later to form a protected inner harbour. The east pier was to be extended in the 1830s, the 1880s and again in the early 1990s.

KIRKWALL HARBOUR.   Kent's "Viking" Series.

15. "KIRKWALL HARBOUR"

This "Kent's 'Viking' Series" postcard shows the east pier on a quiet day when the passers-by have time to stroll, sit or discuss the issues of the moment. The original photograph from which this postcard was printed was probably taken by Tom Kent from one of the upper rooms of the adjacent Kirkwall Hotel. The small harbour office (right) has a notice-board carrying an advertisement for the Highland Railway.

KIRKWALL PIER

16. "KIRKWALL PIER"

Although horses and carts still carry goods to and from the harbour in this later "Leonards 'Orkney' Series" postcard, motorised transport has begun to make its presence felt.

KIRKWALL
HARBOUR STREET

Together with Ayre Road and Shore Street, Harbour Street makes up Kirkwall's main shoreline, with views over Kirkwall Bay. Harbour Street directly faces the piers and the inner harbour and is lined by a number of imposing old buildings.

17. "THE HARBOUR FRONT, KIRKWALL"
Tom Kent's postcard captures a moment in time in a busy Harbour Street. A horse and cart waits outside the St Ola Hotel (centre). The four-storey Kirkwall Hotel (left) was built in 1890 and forms a suitable backdrop to the harbour.

18. "HARBOUR STREET, KIRKWALL"
Photographed at a later date, there is little obvious change in Harbour Street. However, a growing number of motorcars have now replaced horse-drawn vehicles, although not yet in the large numbers to which the modern townscape has had to become accustomed.

KIRKWALL
SHORE STREET AND AYRE ROAD

Postcard publishers always looked for the unusual to help sell their cards to local people and to visitors alike. One 'novelty' as far as the northern isles of Orkney and Shetland are concerned is their long days of virtually continuous daylight at midsummer. Postcards were produced which emphasised the fact that the photograph on the card was taken at midnight.

KIRKWALL FROM CROMWELL'S FORT. (PHOTOGRAPHED AT MIDNIGHT IN MIDSUMMER).

19. "KIRKWALL FROM CROMWELL'S FORT (photographed at midnight in Midsummer)"
Shore Street (centre) has the gable-ends of its rows of seventeenth- and eighteenth-century houses facing Kirkwall Bay. Redevelopment of the area was suggested in the 1920s but the houses were subsequently demolished to make space for an oil depot.

20. "THE AYRE, KIRKWALL, AT MIDNIGHT IN JUNE"
The Ayre Hotel (centre, right) has long been a distinctive feature on Kirkwall's shoreline. The building itself dates back to 1791 when it was originally built on reclaimed land as two separate houses. At the time of this photograph by Tom Kent, the hotel was the "Ayre Temperance Hotel", run by Mr Bisset.

KIRKWALL
BRIDGE STREET

Bridge Street is one of the oldest parts of Kirkwall. At its northern end it is connected with the seafront at Harbour Street. The generally north-south axis of Bridge Street is followed in Albert Street, Broad Street and Victoria Street. This line was originally dictated by the shoreline of the Peerie Sea. Later land reclamation pushed the shoreline well away from the Bridge Street/Victoria Street line and enabled Junction Road and Great Western Road to be built.

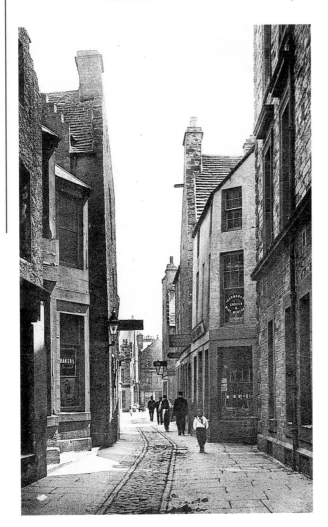

21. "BRIDGE STREET, KIRKWALL"
This "Kent's Series" postcard was printed from a photograph taken in about 1900. It is sub-titled "Where two wheelbarrows tremble when they meet", a quotation from a description of Kirkwall in 1868 and describing the town's narrow streets. The street's central cobbles – which prevented horses' hooves slipping – have been replaced by all-over paving but otherwise this is very much the Bridge Street we see over 90 years later.

22. "BRIDGE STREET, KIRKWALL"
Seen looking northwards towards the harbour, Bridge Street has the typical comings and goings of everyday town life. Although the century was not that well advanced when this postcard was sent from Kirkwall to London in July 1920, it can be seen that the motorcar was beginning to take its place in the town's narrow streets.

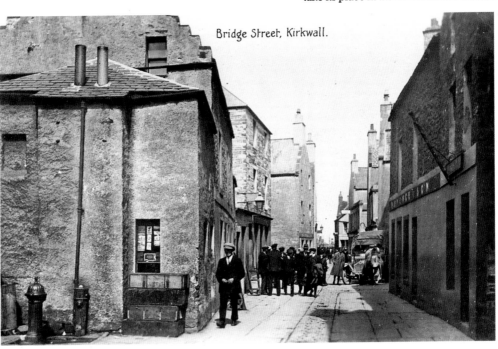

Bridge Street, Kirkwall.

KIRKWALL
ALBERT STREET

Albert Street runs in a north/south direction and has links with Bridge Street and Broad Street. It is Kirkwall's busiest shopping street. Albert Street's famous "Big Tree" (a sycamore) was previously part of a neighbouring private garden. When land was sold to the Burgh Council in the late nineteenth century to allow the street to be widened, a condition of sale stipulated that the tree must be retained.

23. "ALBERT STREET, KIRKWALL"
This WR&S "Reliable Series" postcard shows a quiet moment in what is now one of the town's busiest streets. The Big Tree stands proudly in the thoroughfare. On the left, Stewart's chemist shop has a sign surmounted by a pestle and mortar, emphasising the shopkeeper's trade.

24. "ALBERT STREET, KIRKWALL"
Just a few years later, Tom Kent's real-photograph postcard shows an identical view. The chemist shop now belongs to "Stewart & Heddle" and has a modern shop front. Part of the shop's signs advertise "insurance and family dispensing" and, more mundanely, "sponges".

KIRKWALL
ALBERT STREET AND CASTLE STREET

Albert Street is a street of great charm and character. In too many other towns, old shop frontages have been replaced by the corporate frontages of national chain-stores. In Kirkwall, however, there are still many interesting, locally-owned shops. Many of these still have their gable-ends on the street frontage, retaining the traditional alignment of the houses out of which they have developed.

25. "NAVIGATION UNDER DIFFICULTIES – A WET DAY IN KIRKWALL, 24 SEPTEMBER 1909"
Albert Street ankle-deep in flood-water was one of the consequences of an unusually severe thunderstorm which struck parts of Orkney on 24th September, 1909. Several streets in Kirkwall were flooded when a cloudburst sent a torrent of water cascading through the town. A local man was killed when struck by lightning on the Scapa Road. Tom Kent's postcard was sent from Finstown to Portland, Oregon, USA, on 9th December in the same year.

26. "CASTLE HOTEL, KIRKWALL"
The Castle Hotel was built in 1866 at the junction of Albert Street and Castle Street. The hotel's staff have lined up in Castle Street for what was probably an advertising card for the hotel itself. The plaque above the main door refers to the former site of Kirkwall Castle. The castle had been built in 1380 and its final ruined remains were cleared in 1865 to make way for Castle Street. In more recent years the premises occupied by the Castle Hotel became the local branch of the Trustee Savings Bank. The postcard itself was sent from Kirkwall to Cape Town on 14th December, 1904.

KIRKWALL
BROAD STREET

At its southern end, Albert Street opens out into Broad Street. Together with the adjacent
Kirk Green – which formerly served as Kirkwall's market-place – Broad Street forms a wide expanse,
entirely appropriate to the frontage of St Magnus Cathedral on the east side of the street.

Broad Street, Kirkwall. *Kent's Series.*

27. "BROAD STREET, KIRKWALL"
This early postcard, published by Tom Kent, was posted from Kirkwall to Edinburgh in August
1903. The writer states that, "This is the principal street in Kirkwall" which, in this case, is viewed
looking northwards. Shops such as "John T. Marcus, Flesher" and "J. & W. Tait" line the street and face
St Magnus Cathedral. Towards the right (on the Kirk Green) is the Merkat (Market) Cross on its
three-step plinth. This bears the inscription "1621" but, nevertheless, is thought to be much older.
It has now been replaced by a replica and the original is safely housed in the Cathedral.

Broad Street, Kirkwall

28. "BROAD STREET, KIRKWALL"
To the left on this "Valentine's Series" postcard are the roof-cones and castle-like tower
of the Town Hall. This had been built in 1884 to house the offices of the Burgh Council, the
post office and the public library. It was renovated by the Orkney Islands Council in 1984 to
serve as a community centre. Young trees have newly been planted to flank the Kirk
Green on this postcard and ornamental cannon have been put in place.

KIRKWALL
BROAD STREET

Tom Kent ran his "bookseller" and "stationer" business from premises at 7 Broad Street, where he sold postcards, calendars and a range of fancy goods. The present-day collector of old Orcadian postcards would probably give anything to step back in time to visit Tom Kent's shop. Until his death in 1936, he took a prolific number of photographs of life in Orkney and from them produced a vast number of postcards.

29. "BROAD STREET, KIRKWALL"
Tom Kent's shop is on the right of this "Kent' Series" postcard. A passer-by has paused to look at the array of postcards and other goods on display in the shop window. The shop is today part of "The Longship" premises, selling original Orkney jewellery by Ola Gorie.

30. "BROAD STREET, KIRKWALL"
Tom Kent's shop is in the centre of this later view of Broad Street, which has now become a busier thoroughfare. Behind, the Town Hall dominates this section of the street scene. At this time, Kirkwall's post office was housed in the Town Hall and it is only possible to speculate on the number of picture postcards posted here over the years. A new, replacement post office was built in Junction Road in 1960.

KIRKWALL
WINTERTIME

Snow scenes are relatively uncommon on picture postcards since, if the publishers
are to be believed, skies are always blue and the sun is always shining. This, after all,
is the myth we all like to perpetuate when writing holiday postcards to family and friends.
However, as well as having an eye to the commercial prospects of his postcards, Tom
Kent was keen to record everyday life in Orkney throughout the year.

31. "BROAD STREET, KIRKWALL, IN WINTER"

Tom Kent's superb winter scene shows Broad Street after a snowfall. His own shop is to the right.
The vehicle in the carriageway is a mailcart on its way to the post office at the baronial-style Town Hall
(centre). This postcard was posted from Kirkwall to Dunbar (then Haddington, now Lothian) in 1909. It
has a fine example of a rare Kirkwall postmark, only used for a very short while in March of that year.

32. "KING STREET, KIRKWALL"

King Street runs parallel with Albert Street. Apart from the other qualities of the winter scene
on this "Kent's 'Viking' Series" postcard, it shows that there are in fact plenty of trees in Kirkwall.
The postcard was posted in Kirkwall on 11th December, 1908, and sent to Port of Spain, Trinidad.
It conveyed Christmas and New Year greetings and arrived at its destination on 6th January.

KIRKWALL
ST. MAGNUS CATHEDRAL

St Magnus Cathedral occupies a prominent location in the centre of Kirkwall and is undoubtedly the finest building in Orkney. Although it was constructed over an extended period, it has successfully maintained an architectural unity which has led to it being described as one of the finest and most impressive cathedral churches in Scotland.

ST. MAGNUS CATHEDRAL, FROM POST OFFICE LANE.

33. "ST MAGNUS CATHEDRAL, FROM POST OFFICE LANE"
Post Office Lane was subsequently renamed "St Magnus Lane". This would have been a familiar view to Tom Kent, the postcard's publisher, whose shop was a short distance away in Broad Street.

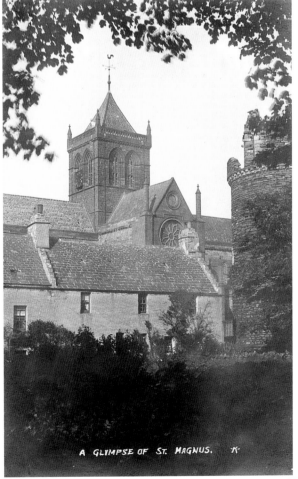

A GLIMPSE OF ST. MAGNUS.

34. "A GLIMPSE OF ST MAGNUS"
This postcard was another from the many views of the cathedral available from Tom Kent's shop. It shows the cathedral's tower and south transept window viewed from the rear of houses in Palace Road. These houses were converted into sheltered housing in the 1970s. The "Moosie Tooer" of the Bishop's Palace appears on the right.

KIRKWALL
ST. MAGNUS CATHEDRAL

Kirkwall's great cathedral was founded in 1137 by Earl Rognvald, Orkney's Norse ruler. It was dedicated to his murdered uncle, St Magnus. Magnus Erlendson had been slain on the island of Egilsay in 1115 by his cousin, Hakon Paulson, with whom he jointly ruled Orkney. Magnus's body was taken to Christ Church, Birsay, where stories soon spread of miraculous cures for those who prayed at the graveside. Rognvald made a vow to build "a stone minster at Kirkwall more magnificent than any in Orkney" to hold Magnus's saintly remains, a vow which helped him take control of the Earldom.

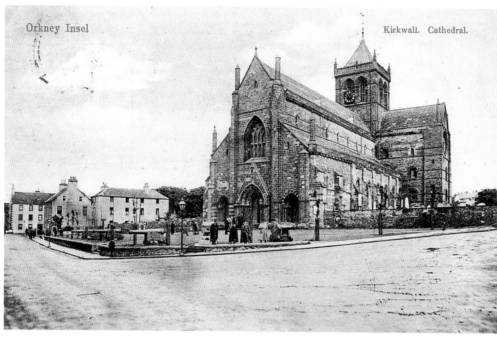

35. "ORKNEY INSEL. KIRKWALL. CATHEDRAL"

The cathedral's western frontage is shown on this unusual postcard bearing an inscription partly in German. It seems likely that a small number of popular pre-1914 postcards might have been printed in this way with European visitors in mind. This card was posted in Kirkwall on 7th August, 1913, and was sent to Thurgau, north-east Switzerland. The message is also written in German.

36. "ST MAGNUS CATHEDRAL FROM E., KIRKWALL"

This hand-coloured "Valentine's Series" postcard shows the opposite view of the cathedral from the preceding postcard. The gravestones which surround the building on three sides might be said to detract from its majestic simplicity but at least serve to show that the cathedral is very much an integral part of the community.

KIRKWALL
ST. MAGNUS CATHEDRAL

Work on St Magnus Cathedral began in 1137 to the design of Rognvald's father, Kol.
It is probable that the stonemasons employed on its construction had previously worked
on Durham Cathedral since many similarities have been noted. In fact, the cathedral in Kirkwall
has been described as "the finest Romanesque work north of Durham". Extensions and alterations
have taken place over the centuries. In 1916, for instance, the short tower seen on Edwardian
picture postcards was replaced by the elegant Gothic spire we see today.

37. "ST MAGNUS CATHEDRAL, KIRKWALL"

The scale and elegance of St Magnus Cathedral (seen here from the west, from the junction of
road Street and Palace Road) is apparent from this later postcard (sent from Kirkwall to Lincoln in
pril 1949). The cathedral celebrated its 850th anniversary in 1987 and the impressive stained-glass
window seen today in the west window dates from this milestone in the building's long history.

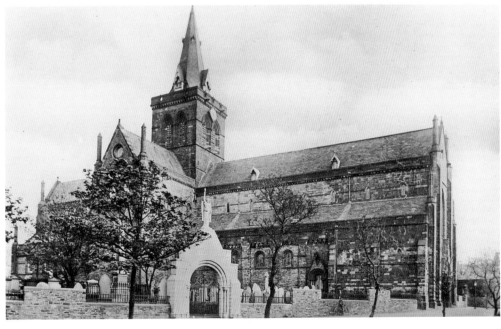

38. "ST MAGNUS CATHEDRAL, KIRKWALL"

This "Kent's Series" postcard shows the view of the cathedral which greets the eye when approaching
from the direction of Albert Street. The parish's dignified war memorial (seen being unveiled in postcard
No. 153) provides a striking gateway through the perimeter wall and into the cathedral's burial ground.

KIRKWALL
ST. MAGNUS CATHEDRAL

St Magnus Cathedral was constructed of rich red sandstone, quarried from the Head of Holland, near Kirkwall. This was skilfully coupled with a yellower stone from Eday, the whole effect being particularly pleasing to the eye. The cathedral we see today is a solid but graceful structure of great warmth and infinite charm. In 1486, King James III gave the cathedral as a gift to the people of Kirkwall. It passed into the ownership of the newly-created Orkney Islands Council in April 1975 and is used as a parish church by the Church of Scotland.

West Doorway, St. Magnus Cathedral, Kirkwall

39. "WEST DOORWAY, ST MAGNUS CATHEDRAL, KIRKWALL"

The three doorways in the cathedral's western elevation date from the thirteenth century when the building was extended. The doorways' arches make use of alternating red and yellow stone, one of the building's pleasing decorative devices.

40. "THE NAVE, ST MAGNUS CATHEDRAL, KIRKWALL"

Whilst restoration works were being undertaken in 1919, a wooden box was found in one of the cathedral's rectangular piers. It contained skeletal remains thought to belong to St Magnus himself. The saint is said to have died of a great blow to the head, and the skull showed evident signs of such a fatal blow.

THE NAVE, ST. MAGNUS CATHEDRAL, KIRKWALL.

KIRKWALL
THE BISHOP'S PALACE

The Bishop's Palace is located at the junction of Palace Road and Watergate. The building's earliest stonework suggests that the Bishops of Orkney moved their residence from Birsay to Kirkwall when work began on the adjacent cathedral in 1137. It is reasonable to assume that the palace was built by William the Old, the Norse Bishop of Orkney during the 66 years between 1102 and 1168. The palace building was to be altered substantially over the following centuries.

41. "THE BISHOP'S PALACE, KIRKWALL"
Looking westwards along Palace Road, the boundary wall of St Magnus Cathedral is on the right and the prominent "Moosie Tooer" – the round tower of the Bishop's Palace, on the Palace Road frontage – is on the left. The tower itself dates from about 1550.

42. "THE BISHOP'S PALACE, KIRKWALL"
The trees on the left are in the grounds of the Sheriff's Court. The road running between the Courthouse and the Bishop's Palace is known as "Watergate", named after the walled archway which spanned the road at this junction until removed as part of a road-widening scheme in 1877. As shown on this postcard by David Spence, the Watergate itself was preserved by rebuilding it into the outer wall of the Bishop's Palace.

KIRKWALL
THE BISHOP'S PALACE

Most of what can be seen of the Bishop's Palace today dates back to the mid-sixteenth century. The Palace had become ruinous in the fourteenth century but was repaired and extended by Bishop Robert Reid in the period 1554-85. Part of his additions was the high, round "Moosie Tooer". The fact that the Bishop's Palace was built to resemble a fortified castle is probably indicative of the troubled times in which Bishop Reid lived.

43. "ST MAGNUS CATHEDRAL AND BISHOP'S PALACE, KIRKWALL"

This early "Valentine's Series" postcard shows the view looking northwards along Watergate. The stonework of the Bishop's Palace is on the left and the south transept of St Magnus Cathedral is straight ahead. The grounds of the Sheriff's Court are on the right.

44. "INTERIOR OF BISHOP'S PALACE AND CATHEDRAL TOWER, KIRKWALL"

The interior of the Bishop's Palace was altered at various times over its long history but today, as this postcard shows, it is ruinous and it is not easy to visualise the scale of the store-rooms on the ground floor and the great hall and other apartments on the upper floors. The spire of St Magnus Cathedral rises up beyond, on the other side of Palace Road.

KIRKWALL
THE EARL'S PALACE

The Earl's Palace is situated in Palace Road, a few steps away from the Bishop's Palace.
It was built for Patrick Stewart, the controversial Earl of Orkney, early in the seventeenth
century and has been described as "One of the finest Renaissance palaces in Scotland".
Though now ruined, it is relatively easy to get a clear impression of the building's
original scale and magnificence. It has been in the care of the state since 1920.

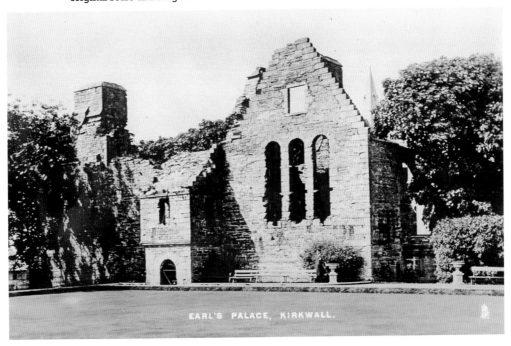

EARL'S PALACE, KIRKWALL.

45. "EARL'S PALACE, KIRKWALL"

The triple-arched window in the palace's southern elevation gave light to its great hall,
which had the imposing dimensions of 20 by 55 feet. Part of the palace grounds had been
turned into a bowling green by the time this photograph was taken. It was published as a
postcard for David Spence, the Kirkwall stationer, by Raphael Tuck & Sons of London.

46. "EARL'S PALACE, KIRKWALL"

The scale of the Earl's Palace is apparent from this anonymously-published postcard showing
three children looking up in awe at the great corner turrets and striking corbelling. Patrick Stewart,
Earl of Orkney, didn't manage to enjoy the pleasures of this magnificent palace for long. He
was arrested in 1609 and executed in Edinburgh in 1615 on a charge of treason.

BROAD STREET AND VICTORIA STREET

At the head of Broad Street, near its junction with Palace Road and Victoria Street,
Tankerness House Museum can be found. Just to the south, Victoria Street itself has a
street-scene which still retains many of the characteristic frontages of former times.

47. "HEAD OF BROAD STREET, KIRKWALL"

David Spence sold postcards from his bookseller and stationer's business at premises (centre left) at
the head of Broad Street. The building itself had a long and varied history but was demolished in 1930
to create a wider vehicular access to Victoria Street (centre). The arched gateway to Tankerness House
(right) bears the date 1574. For many years this house was the town house of the Baikies of Tankerness
but was restored by Orkney Islands Council in 1968 and now houses an excellent museum.

48. "VICTORIA STREET, KIRKWALL"

Victoria Street continues the north/south line established by Albert Street and Broad Street.
To this day it remains a narrow and irregular street with many of its properties showing their
gable-ends to the street frontage. The shop premises in the right foreground of this postcard
are occupied by *The Orcadian*, the islands' own local newspaper (founded in 1854).

KIRKWALL

For such a relatively small town, Kirkwall has a wealth of architectural interest
Much of it has been captured on picture postcards over the years. With or without
a guidebook, a stroll through the town, tracking down the locations of a century
of picture postcards, can be a fascinating and rewarding experience.

49. "THE BURGH SCHOOL, KIRKWALL"

Kirkwall Grammar School had occupied this site in School Place since 1820. The buildings shown
on this "Kent's Series" postcard date from about 1890 and would have housed about 600 pupils. Later,
in 1980, the former school buildings were converted to serve as the offices of the Orkney Islands
Council. Replacement primary and secondary schools were purpose-built elsewhere in the town.

50. "HIGHLAND PARK, NEAR KIRKWALL"

Tom Kent's postcard, sent from Kirkwall to London in June 1924, shows what is now Highland
Park House, a residential home situated behind the famous whisky distillery that bears the same
name. Highland Park, Britain's northernmost whisky distillery, was founded in the 1790s. It has an
excellent visitor centre. Orkney's second distillery, overlooking Scapa Flow, dates from the 1880s.

Visits to Kirkwall Bay by British and other fleets used to be quite commonplace. Visiting naval personnel added to the life and vigour of the town. In 1912, the Admiralty officially designated Scapa Flow as a naval anchorage and, as a result, the sight of flotillas anchored in Kirkwall Bay itself became rarer.

51. "1st DESTROYER FLOTILLA, KIRKWALL BAY. ILLUMINATED 27 MAY 1911"
The 1st Destroyer Flotilla included *HMS Amazon*, *HMS Blenheim*, *HMS Swift*,
HMS Tartar and the cruiser *HMS Blanche*. The flotilla's night-time
illuminations provided a spectacular display for the residents of Kirkwall.

52. "REGATTA 1st DESTROYER FLOTILLA, KIRKWALL
FANCY DRESS BOAT FIRST PRIZE HMS JACKAL"
Visits by naval flotillas were not necessarily all pomp and circumstance. The naval
personnel themselves appreciated the chance to enjoy shore-leave after weeks at
sea and, on such occasions, light-hearted fun and frivolity was the other of the day.

SPECIAL OCCASIONS
THE BA'

The Ba' is played through the streets of Kirkwall on Christmas Day and New Year's Day.
Although it resembles mass football games played elsewhere in Britain, its origins are unknown.
The game's contestants form two huge teams. From the starting points at the site of the Merkat
Cross, the "Down-the-gates" team (or "Doonies") (those born south of the east/west dividing
line) endeavour to get the ba' (ball) northwards and into the harbour. The "Up-the-gates"
("Uppies") strive to take the ba' southwards to a point known as Mackinson's Corner.

53. "KIRKWALL NEW YEAR'S DAY BA' 1909"
Tom Kent produced a series of postcards of the Christmas and New Year's Ba'. On sale at his Broad Street
shop within a few days, he could rely on a significant sale to those who could recognise themselves or
their family or friends in the crowd. This particular postcard was sent from Kirkwall to Perth on 7th
January, 1909, and included the message, "Find on other side two men you know".

54. "MEN'S BA', KIRKWALL, CHRISTMAS 1921"
Twelve years later, Tom Kent stood at much the same spot (looking northwards along Broad Street) to
take this photograph of the Christmas Ba'. The sender of the postcard writes, "... just have a look to see
how many you know. You can just see my back ... Ethel & Bena Corsie quite plain".

Coronation Day celebrations for King George V and Queen Mary were held throughout Orkney in June, 1911. In Kirkwall itself, the celebrations began with a civic service in St Magnus Cathedral. The Coronation was an occasion for decorating the streets and dressing in Sunday-best clothing.

55. "SCHOOL CHILDREN MARCHING TO BIGNOLD PARK 23.6.11"
Tom Kent photographed the children's parade at the head of Broad Street on its way up
to Victoria Street toward Bignold Park where a programme of events had been drawn up.
The post office and shop premises of John T. Marcus and J. & W. Tait are all bedecked with
flags and bunting. This postcard was sent from Kirkwall to Thurso just ten days later.

56. "CYCLE PARADE, CORONATION DAY, KIRKWALL"
In the evening of Coronation Day, a fancy-dress cycle parade took place. Almost 100 cyclists assembled
in Broad Street where judging took place. The contestants then paraded through Kirkwall's streets.

ORCADIANS

In the year of the first census of population (1801) there were 24,445 people living in Orkney. The islands reached their maximum population in 1861, with 32,200 inhabitants. With the islands' natural resources unable to provide for such a large population, emigration became a feature of island life. Over 4,000 islanders contributed to the net emigration figures in each decade during the 1860s, '80s and '90s, with Orcadians setting out for a new life on the British mainland or in Britain's overseas dominions.

57. "AN ORKNEY ELOPEMENT"
In the "golden age" of picture postcards, comic cards were universally popular and widely collected throughout Britain. Tom Kent produced his own comic cards. "An Orkney Elopement" was the humorous title given to this postcard showing two young Orcadians enjoying a leisurely time with their two ponies.

58. "WEARY WILLIE OF THE ORKNEYS"
"Weary Willie" was much photographed by Tom Kent and a number of different postcards were produced from these photographs. William Laughton – nicknamed "Skatehorn" – was a wandering eccentric at the turn of the century. It is thought that he was born in Aberdeenshire and had come to Orkney as a pedlar. Although he spent most of his life on the open road, he died in the local county home.

Life in Orkney has often been hard and so work itself had to be taken seriously. Leisure time, therefore, was a precious commodity and had to be taken equally as seriously. Women's and young people's groups, church societies and other social groups have been active in the islands for many years.

59. "KIRKWALL BOYS' BRIGADE IN CAMP AT ORPHIR. FILLING THE BEDS"
The young members of Kirkwall's Boys' Brigade are obviously participating in
an organised outing to an outdoor camp in this postcard by J. Omond. At a farmhouse
in Orphir parish they are filling their bedding-bags with straw from the farmer's
hay-stack. It might be rather basic but was probably great fun.

60. "CAMP OF ORKNEY TERRITORIALS, KIRKWALL 20.8.09"
When the Orkney branch of the Territorial Army set up its training camp on the outskirts
of Kirkwall in August 1909, Tom Kent was there to record the event. Such postcards,
depicting special events in the town, would have been available for sale very shortly
after the event took place. In the days before mass-circulation newspapers, postcards of
this type were often the only photographic record available to the public in general.

THE ORKNEY FARMHOUSE

Crofting has long been the economic mainstay of life in Orkney. Until the twentieth century brought its technological advances, farming in the islands had largely remained unchanged over many centuries. The centre of the crofters' life was the family home, a simple, stone-built farmhouse which owed much to the design of the traditional viking longhouse.

The Crofter's Home, Orkney

61. "THE CROFTER'S HOME, ORKNEY"

This hand-coloured "Kent's Series" postcard shows a typical Orkney farmhouse with its thatched roof and range of outbuildings. Using basic agricultural implements, the crofter grew oats and bere (barley), used seaweed to manure the fields and kept chickens, pigs and one or two cows. The cows were kept to supply the family's milk, butter and cheese.

Primitive Cottage, near Stromness

Valentine's Series, "Crystoleum." Patent applied for. 23,063

62. "PRIMITIVE COTTAGE, NEAR STROMNESS"

An even earlier and more "primitive" farmhouse is shown in this early postcard. It clearly shows the turfed or thatched roof construction, held down with thick ropes and flagstones to prevent damage during the winter gales. The byre, or cattle-shed, was a continuation of the two-roomed dwellinghouse, and cattle and humans entered by the same door. The crofthouse had a central hearth and smoke from the peat fire found its way through the hole in the roof.

THE ORKNEY FARMHOUSE

The hard-won fruits of the crofter's labours on the land were seldom sufficient to ensure the family's well-being. The men's endeavours had to be supplemented by fishing and, in some parts of Orkney, by collecting seabirds' eggs from the cliffs. The women spent hours spinning, knitting woollen garments and making linen cloth. In earlier years, many crofters also helped the lairds accrue wealth from the local kelp industry.

63. "INTERIOR OF AN ORKNEY COTTAGE"
The original photograph for this "Kent's Series" postcard was taken in about 1900. It shows the interior of Netherby, a farmhouse in Deerness, the easternmost parish on Mainland. The spinning wheels, straw-backed chairs and box beds with sliding doors show the typical contents of most farmhouses at this time.

64. "ROUND THE ORKNEY PEAT FIRE"
This lovely postcard study of the interior of Kirbuster farmhouse in Birsay sadly has no photographer's or publisher's name. It shows that most farmhouses, with their bare flagstoned floors and simple, straight-backed chairs, had few of the creature comforts we now take for granted. The central, peat-fired hearth was used for all the family's cooking. Kirbuster is now preserved as a museum.

THE ORKNEY FARMHOUSE

Farming techniques in Orkney have improved beyond all recognition during the twentieth century. The average size of agricultural units in the islands almost doubled in the forty years after 1945, leading to increased mechanism and productivity. Previously unproductive upland areas have now been reclaimed and Orkney is now probably greener than it ever was. Along with these changes, however, has come a decline in the numbers employed in agriculture and, consequently, a significant depopulation of Orkney's rural areas.

65. "THE INGLE NOOK, ORKNEY"

This postcard was printed from a photograph taken by Tom Kent in about 1900. It is known to be the interior of Burness House, a two-storey farmhouse in the parish of Firth. Apart from the inglenook itself – which was quite an unusual feature in Orkney farmhouses – the interior shows many features commonly found in houses at this time, including the fish and meat hanging to cure from the ceiling.

66. "THE LIGHT OF OTHER DAYS. ORKNEY CRUSIES"

Crusie lamps were commonly used in Orkney farmhouses up to the mid-nineteenth century. They would have been made by the local blacksmith. The upper part held a small reservoir of oil and could be adjusted to give an even flow of the oil to the cotton wick at the front. The lower part caught any drips.

A LIVING FROM THE LAND
PEAT FOR FUEL

Peat, a material typical of cool, damp climates, is one of Orkney's most abundant raw materials. For centuries, it was the most common domestic fuel used in both town and country. The cutting process would start in the spring and would proceed until the crofter assessed that he had cut sufficient peat to last the family throughout the coming winter and right through to the next peat-cutting season.

67. "CUTTING PEATS"
Once the covering turf had been removed and the peat bank exposed, the process of cutting could begin, a task often undertaken communally. Using a narrow spade, each peat slab would be carefully laid on top of the peat bank to form a small wall. A few days later the peat blocks would be raised into small, regular mounds to aid the drying process.

68. "CARTING HOME THE PEATS, BIRSAY"
When the drying process was finally complete, the peats had to be transported back home using whatever methods were available. The tractor and trailer is now the normal means but, in the past, wheelbarrows might be used or, where available, a horse or an ox would pull the laden cart. Carting home the peats was an important event in the crofting year. Like the one above, this postcard was printed from a photograph taken in about 1900.

A LIVING FROM THE LAND
AGRICULTURE

Oats and bere (a variety of barley) were the main crops grown on the islands' better soils but methods of cultivation remained both labour-intensive and back-breaking well into the twentieth century. Ploughing and harrowing the soil, sewing the seed, reaping the ripened crops and grinding the grains were all vital stages in the agricultural year, and the family's well-being depended on the successful completion of each stage.

Ploughing with Oxen (Woman)

69. "PLOUGHING THE OXEN (WOMAN)"

Sent from Finstown to Portland, Oregon, in October 1910, this postcard was published by George Washington Wilson from a photograph taken in about 1890. The postcard's title seems to suggest that it was quite unusual to see a woman performing the heavy task of ploughing. However, it was probably not an uncommon sight in Orkney's crofting communities.

70. "STRANGE WORKMATES"

The "strange workmates" in this anonymously-published postcard are a horse and an ox, yoked together to pull a wooden plough.

A LIVING FROM THE LAND
AGRICULTURE

Edwardian picture postcards from Orkney often show oxen used as beasts of
burden. Cattle are shown harnessed to ploughs or pulling carts. This is a reflection
both of the relatively primitive nature of Orcadian agriculture and the fact that
cattle were more important than horses to Orkney's crofting community.

71. "A HORSELESS CARRIAGE"
The "horseless carriage" in Tom Kent's postcard was not a motorcar but one of the islands' bullock carts.
These carts were used for numerous purposes in the everyday life of Orkney's crofting communities
The most famous of Orkney's bullock carts was the "Hoy Express" (postcard No. 167) which was
used by the Post Office to convey the mails over the rough moorland tracks of the island of Hoy.

72. "THE ORKNEY CROFTER'S STEED"
Apart from the other uses to which it could be put, the ox-drawn cart could
save enormous human toil in carrying seaweed from the shore to the fields. The
seaweed itself was used as a simple and free fertiliser, rich in natural minerals.

A LIVING FROM THE LAND
AGRICULTURE

Harvest is an important time for all farming communities. Before the days of convenience shopping, the crofter was reliant on what could be produced on the land. Grain-crops were needed to feed the family until the following year's harvest and fodder crops were needed to feed the animals during the winter months. Rents had to be paid from whatever sources were available and small surpluses could be used to obtain luxury goods such as tea and tobacco.

CARTING HAY IN THE ORKNEYS   W. H.

73. "CARTING HAY IN THE ORKNEYS"
Published from a photograph taken on Hoy by William Hourston in about 1920, this postcard shows crofters forking hay onto a four-wheeled Orkney "sled".

GRINDING OATS WITH THE QUERN ORKNEY

Kent's "Viking" Series

74. "GRINDING OATS WITH THE QUERN"
The quern, or hand-mill, is thought to have been introduced to Britain by the Romans. It became an indispensible implement on virtually every Orkney croft and was still widely in use at the beginning of the twentieth century. The lower of the two circular stones was static whilst the upper one was rotated by means of a wooden handle. Using this laborious process, small quantities of grain, fed through the central hole, would be ground for domestic use.

There were few occasions when the Orkney farmers' hands were idle. The need to ensure the family's well-being meant that there were always tasks to be undertaken in the fields or in the home. Spinning, for instance, was a traditional craft and provided welcome additional income for the family. The spinning of wool was not such a major enterprise as it was in Shetland and, instead, flax – grown in Orkney – was at one time more important, reaching a peak in the early years of the nineteenth century. The task of spinning flax into yarn required great skill.

75. "GATHERING POTATOES, ORPHIR"
Potatoes had first been grown as a field crop in Orkney in about 1750 and were to become a widespread crop after a hurricane damaged the corn crop in 1756. Potatoes became the family's staple diet at those times of year when meal grew scarce and could be expected to feature in the morning, midday and evening meals. This particular "Kent's Series" postcard was sent from Stromness to North Ronaldsay, Orkney's northernmost island, in May 1909.

76. "SPINNING, ORKNEY"
Sent from Evie to Leith in October 1908, this postcard was part of the "Leonard's Orkney Series". The spinning wheel shown is the traditional horizontal type, used for spinning wool. This was larger than the vertical type, which was usually used for the spinning of flax.

A LIVING FROM THE LAND
ORKNEY CHAIRS

The making of Orkney chairs – or "stools" – is a traditional local craft. Happily, the skill required to make these beautiful chairs has survived to this day. The chairs – made of woven straw and, traditionally, items of driftwood – were a common feature in the Orkney crofthouse. There were often different sizes and designs for men, women and children.

77. "MAKING STRAW-BACKED CHAIRS"
The croft of Nessie in Tankerness parish was the location for Tom Kent's photograph from which this postcard was printed. Robert Foubister is seen making the chair whilst his daughter, Lizzie, cleans the straw used in the chair-making process.

78. "CHAIR-MAKING"
This "Leonard's Orkney Series" postcard was sent from Kirkwall to Portsmouth in June 1909. Part of the message read, "I wonder if you'd like a chair like this. They are only 18/6d. The King bought one and several other members of the Royal Family. They are very comfortable indeed to sit in".

A LIVING FROM THE LAND
FOWLING AND KELPING

Orkney's long coastline provided an additional means of livelihood for many crofters.
For some, the islands' great cliffs provided seasonal harvests of seabirds and their eggs.
In addition, the abundance of seaweed on Orkney's shores was harvested, either as
a fertiliser or, for many years, to be burnt for the commercial value of its ash.

Cliff Climbing for Wild Fowl Eggs. Orkney.

79. "CLIFF-CLIMBING FOR WILD FOWL EGGS"

Fowling was a skilled but dangerous art. It was once common to the great cliffs of both Orkney and Shetland. On remote St Kilda, this skill was the mainstay of the islanders' life prior to the island's evacuation in 1930. Birds' eggs would be taken for food direct from the cliff ledges. The birds themselves were also caught and their meat used for food, feathers for pillows and bones as fertiliser.

80. "BURNING KELP, BIRSAY"

Kelp production was a major industry in Orkney during the eighteenth century. It was prepared by burning tangles (seaweed) in circular, stone-lined pits or 'kelp-kilns', and was used in the manufacture of soap, iodine and glass. Kelp had first been produced in Orkney in the 1720s and, in its heyday, the industry employed about 3,000 people in the islands. The industry reached a peak in 1825 but declined thereafter. Remnants of the industry still remained when George Washington Wilson visited Orkney in the early 1890s and took the photograph at Birsay from which this postcard was printed.

A LIVING FROM THE SEA

Although farming has traditionally been the Orcadian's chief means of livelihood, there has
been an age-old tradition of earning at least a part-time living from the sea. This pattern existed
for centuries but, for a period at the end of the nineteenth century and the beginning of the twentieth,
the herring boom – especially at Stromness and on the islands of Stronsay, Burray and South
Ronaldsay – seemed to suggest that fishing might replace farming as the main way of life.

KENT'S ORCADIAN SERIES.

81. "STROMNESS IN FISHING TIME"

This multi-view postcard shows Stromness during its busy herring-fishing season. The town had become
Orkney's major fishing port by 1898 and its normal population of about 2,000 temporarily trebled with
the annual influx of fishermen, gutters, curers and packers from the ports of north and north-east
Scotland. By 1908 the main centre of Orkney's herring fishing had moved to the island of Stronsay.

82. "FISH AUCTION MART, STRONSAY"

Whitehall – Stronsay's main settlement – became one of Scotland's major herring ports.
During the industry's heyday, it employed thousands of men, women and children in Whitehall
and, for the few weeks of the herring season in July and August, up to 400 boats crowded the
harbour. Whitehall's fish market, built at the pierhead in the early twentieth century, was the
busiest of places every Tuesday morning for these few weeks. The industry declined during the
1930s when modern fishing methods began to deplete the once-prosperous fishing grounds.

STROMNESS

Stromness is Orkney's second town and, in terms of the islands' links with the
Scottish mainland, its chief ferry port. Its deep and sheltered bay – Hamnavoe – has
been an important anchorage for many centuries. The town occupies the long, narrow
coastal strip beneath the hill known as Brinkie's Brae (390 feet). Its main street curves
and winds along the contours of the bay. It is a town of great charm and character.

83. "STROMNESS"

The publishers known by the trade-name "Ja-Ja"
produced an extensive "Heraldic Series" of postcards
depicting the badges and crests of British towns. This
particular postcard shows the Stromness Burgh badge with
its stylised viking longship and its Latin motto "Per Mare".

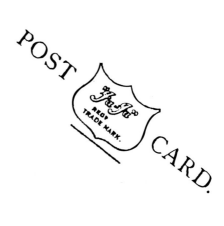

84. "STROMNESS FROM NORTH"

Herring boats crowd Stromness harbour in this early
"Valentine's Series" postcard. This view of the town is from
Brinkie's Brae, the hill which provides the western backdrop.
Almost the whole of Stromness can be seen in this panoramic
view, right down to the Point of Ness. The shoreline of the
Point of Ness was the main focus of the town's herring
fishing boom between 1893 and the First World War.

STROMNESS

Britain's long wars between the late seventeenth and the early nineteenth centuries
proved to be beneficial to Stromness. Shipping ran the risk of enemy attack if using the English
Channel and so preferred the longer but safer route round the North of Scotland. With its sheltered
bay, Stromness was a convenient place for re-provisioning and the town's trade grew accordingly.

85. "STROMNESS FROM NORTH, LOOKING TO HOY"
It is relatively uncommon to see British picture postcards with the stamp and postmark on the front,
whereas it was a common practice in many European countries. The sender of this particular postcard
was French and the postcard itself was sent to the village of Lambezellec (now part of Brest) in Brittany.

86. "AN APRIL DAY IN THE ORKNEYS"
Stromness, with its majestic backdrop of the snow-clad hills of Hoy, is seen mirrored in the calm
waters of Hamnavoe in this postcard by William Hourston. Stromness came to be William Hourston's
adopted home, and he took many fine photographs of the area right up to the late 1950s.

STROMNESS

The success of sea-borne trade for Stromness was such that for a short while at the beginning of the nineteenth century its population was probably slightly greater than that of Kirkwall. Sailing ships bound for Canada or for the whaling seas of the north made Stromness their final port of call. Ships of the Hudson Bay Company re-provisioned and recruited at Stromness between the 1670s and the 1890s.

87. "STROMNESS FROM BRINKIE'S BRAE"
A walk to the top of Brinkie's Brae is rewarded by this magnificent panoramic view of Stromness. This postcard by William Hourston looks across the waters to the hills of Hoy. In between is the small island of Graemsay. The tall white tower of Hoy Lighthouse (postcard No. 163), one of Graemsay's two lighthouses, is seen on the upper left.

88. "STROMNESS HARBOUR AND THE HOLMS"
"The Holms" are the two small tidal islands, Inner Holm and Outer Holm, which form the eastern boundary of Stromness harbour. In this particular view, the sheltered waters are providing anchorage for a large warship whilst the Scrabster-Stromness ferry, *St Ola*, glides gently past.

STROMNESS

At the height of its commercial success, Stromness was elevated to Burgh status in 1817. The town's population was about 2,200 at this time. As the century progressed and as sailing ships gave way to steam-powered vessels, the importance of Stromness began to decline. Its population had fallen to about 1,400 by 1961 but was to increase again as new housing developments were built in the 1970s. The town's Burgh status came to an end in 1975 with the establishment of the Orkney Islands Council.

89. "STROMNESS FROM THE SOUTH"
This was one of Tom Kent's most popular postcards. Printed from a photograph taken in about 1910, it shows Stromness from the South End with Brinkie's Brae rising up behind. The seashore has served as a playground for generations of Stromness children.

90. "STROMNESS FROM NESS ROAD"
"Had a great thrill coming up in the plane at about 120 miles an hour", wrote the sender of this postcard in July 1936 to an address in Inverness. The first regular Inverness-Kirkwall flight had been started by Highland Airways in May 1933. The airline's bi-planes were small and relatively few visitors would have arrived in Orkney by air in the 1930s.

STROMNESS

As opportunities for trade increased, merchants built their houses along the Stromness shoreline. Many houses had small slipways allowing boats to be launched into the harbour. As the town grew, housing spread along the edges of the bay and, where feasible, up the slopes of the hills providing protection for the town from the westerly winds.

91. "STROMNESS FROM THE SEA"

This postcard bears the embossed name of "W. Hourston" in the lower left-hand corner. This face-on view of the town must have been a familiar sight to William Hourston. On the left is the spire of the former Free Church of Scotland (now serving as the Town Hall) and, behind it, is the former parish church of St Peter's (now a community centre). In the background is Stromness School (postcard No. 109).

92. "A BIT OF OLD STROMNESS"

John Rae sold this postcard from his bookseller and stationer's shop in Victoria Street, Stromness. The houses in the centre have access to both the sea and the town's main street and are entirely characteristic of practically the entire length of the town's waterfront.

STROMNESS
"A NORTHERN VENICE"

Postcard publishers often called Stromness "A Northern Venice". The same romantic description was often given to Lerwick, Shetland's main town, to which it bears a strong resemblance. The houses, shops and storage facilities hugging the shoreline and the large number of small piers and slipways, all emphasise the age-old relationship between Stromness and the sea.

93. "STROMNESS, ORKNEY. A NORTHERN VENICE"
This attractive, hand-coloured "Valentine's Series" postcard was printed from a photograph taken from Sutherland's Pier. Perhaps detracting from the romantic imagery of "a northern Venice", the semi-circular structure built into the sea-wall to the left of centre is actually a corrugated iron toilet, suspended over the sea! Local sewerage arrangements were to be improved in the years just before the First World War.

94. "STROMNESS. 'A NORTHERN VENICE'"
John Rae's superb photographic postcard shows Stromness mirrored in the waters of Hamnavoe. This is the same stretch of waterfront shown on the preceding postcard. It demonstrates the complex elevations and roof-lines which make Stromness such an attractive town.

John Rae, Stationer, Stromness

The character of Stromness has changed little over the twentieth century. Many views of the town depicted on picture postcards in the "golden age" of postcard production would be instantly recognisable today. When conservation began to replace demolition as the cornerstone of British urban life, the importance of the heritage of Stromness was recognised. A large part of the town's core area has been designated a Conservation Area.

95. "A BIT OF OLD STROMNESS"

Baskets, packing boxes and rowing boats in this postcard by R. W. Clouston are all reminders of the townsfolk's traditional reliance on fishing. Taking advantage of the day's sunshine, a heavy wash has been hung to dry at the water's edge at what is now known as Flaw's Pier. This was originally the Watch Quay of the Stromness pilots, who drew up their boats beside it on the Broad Noust.

This is a Real Photograph

96. "IN PURSUIT OF THE GENTLE ART, STROMNESS"

The "gentle art" in this postcard published for L. J. Smith, Stromness, is the skill of fishing for sillocks (young saithe) without having to leave your own home! The postcard, showing a part of the town to the rear of Dundas Street, was published from an earlier photograph by George Washington Wilson, taken in about 1890.

STROMNESS

Arrival at Stromness on the modern roll-on/roll-off ferry takes the traveller past the slipways and jetties scattered along the shoreline and straight into the heart of the town itself. The pierhead always seems to be the busiest of places when the ferry arrives or departs.

97. "OFF IN THE MORNING, STROMNESS"
The first ship to be named *St Ola* gave a lifetime's service to the North Company's Scrabster-Stromness route. She first appeared at Stromness in 1892 and was to be a regular and welcome visitor to the town for almost 60 years until her deserved retirement in 1951.

98. "THE PIER HEAD, STROMNESS"
This postcard, published by R. W. Clouston, shows a view of the pierhead which would be instantly recognisable today. The harbour is often busy with vessels of all sizes and you can invariably see rather more than a solitary rowing boat! The Stromness Hotel dominates the other buildings at the pierhead.

STROMNESS
STROMNESS HOTEL

On arrival at the pierhead, one of the first landmarks likely to be noticed is the imposing facade of the four-storey, stone-built Stromness Hotel. The building dates from 1901. During the Second World War it was requisitioned by the military forces to serve as the Orkney and Shetland Defence Headquarters. Perhaps the most famous visitor at this time was Gracie Fields, who entertained the troops by singing from the hotel's balcony.

99. "STROMNESS HOTEL"
The hotel's front facade bears the letters "MACKAY'S STROMNESS HOTEL" in this "Valentine's Series" postcard. John Mackay owned the hotel, having financed its construction. He also owned the Standing Stones Hotel in Stenness (postcard No. 129).

100. "STROMNESS HOTEL FROM THE PIER"
Boxes awaited collection at the pierhead in this later postcard, published by L. J. Smith of Stromness. A bus waits outside the Stromness Hotel, probably having arrived from Kirkwall. The offices of "The North of Scotland & Orkney & Shetland Steam Navigation Company Ltd" (The North Company) are on the right.

STROMNESS
VICTORIA STREET

One long, winding, flagstoned main street runs the entire north/south length of
Stromness. From John Street, at its northern end, the main street in turn becomes
Victoria Street, Graham Place, Dundas Street, Alfred Street and South End before leaving
Stromness as Ness Road. The road meanders as it parallels the town's shoreline.

101. "VICTORIA STREET, STROMNESS"

This animated street scene shows a busy Victoria Street
with goods for sale and passers-by apparently in their finest
attire. It is possible that the postcard shows Stromness during
its annual Lammas Fair. Held on the first Tuesday in
September, this was the greatest annual event in Stromness
before the Second World War. The postcard was sent from
Dounby to Leek, Staffordshire, in October 1910.

VICTORIA STREET, STROMNESS, ORKNEY. PHOTO D.R.G.B.

102. "VICTORIA STREET, STROMNESS"

The narrowness of Victoria Street is apparent from this
postcard. On the left is the draper's shop of John G. Johnston.
The carriage awaits outside the Commercial Hotel. On the
right, Robert H. Robertson's grocery shop advertised
"Melrose's Teas". Beyond was the Mason's Arms Hotel.

Victoria Street
Stromness.

STROMNESS

VICTORIA STREET AND GRAHAM PLACE

Victoria Street has long been the town's main commercial thoroughfare. Amongst its other premises, it is the location of the town's post office (at 37 Victoria Street). A post office opened in Stromness in 1797, about 50 years after Orkney's first post office, in Kirkwall. At its southern end, Victoria Street leads into Graham Place which, although quieter, is still busy with the comings and goings of town life.

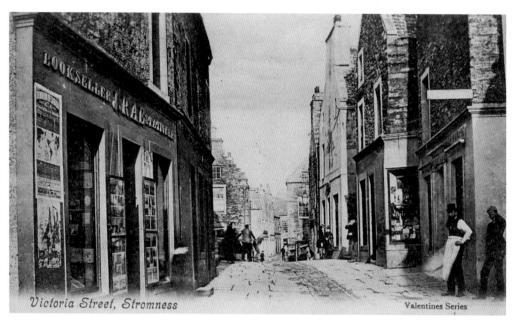

103. "VICTORIA STREET, STROMNESS"

On the left are the shop premises of John Rae ("bookseller and stationer"). The shop sold a wide range of items including picture postcards, as can be seen from the racks hanging on either side of the door. John Rae himself later published many fine local postcards in his own name. An advertisement for the "Dominion of Canada" in the upper left illustrates that Rae's shop acted as a booking agency for shipping companies involved with emigration from Britain. The shop is still trading today.

104. "GRAHAM PLACE, STROMNESS"

Graham Place was named after Alexander Graham who, in the years after 1743, led local merchants in a long and ultimately successful campaign to end the special taxes which Stromness businesses were obliged to pay to Kirkwall. A commemorative plaque to Graham's memory is to be found on the fountain at the pierhead.

STROMNESS
DUNDAS STREET

Dundas Street is the narrowest and most picturesque part of the town's main street and, as such,
it attracted the attention of the publishers of picture postcards from the earliest days. As the town grew
and as housing spread westwards up the hillsides, the new houses were linked to the main street by
a series of steep and narrow closes. One of these bears the appropriate name of "Khyber Pass".

105. "DUNDAS STREET, STROMNESS"
"No room for motors", wrote the sender of this postcard in August 1904, "nothing wider than a small cart can go along". The postcard was printed from a photograph taken by George Washington Wilson in about 1890. The men on the left are standing outside one of the town's public houses.

106. "DUNDAS STREET, STROMNESS"
This view of Dundas Street, dating from the early years of the twentieth century and looking northwards towards Graham Place, is largely recognisable today. Shop signs such as "J. Hobbs. Lodgings & Refreshments" may have altered and motorised transport has replaced the handcart but, otherwise, a stroll along Dundas Street today would evoke strong memories of this by-gone moment in time.

STROMNESS

Although Stromness has a great feeling of timelessness, time itself has not stood still and there have been many changes in the town over the years. Whisky lovers will probably lament the loss of the town's distillery which closed in the early years of the twentieth century. An attractive housing development was later built on the site of the distillery.

Queen Street, Stromness. *Thanks! Best wishes* RELIABLE WH&S SERIES.

107. "QUEEN STREET, STROMNESS"
Sent from Stromness to Kettering in June 1903, this early, undivided-back postcard shows a view of houses in Queen Street. Most of the houses still have their traditional flagstone roofs covered with straw ropes ("simmens"). Many of these particular houses were demolished in 1911 and incorporated into Back Road.

STROMNESS TOWN CRIER.
(From Photo. taken on occasion of Diamond Jubilee of Queen Victoria, 1897.)

108. "STROMNESS TOWN CRIER"
The Town Crier in this anonymously-published postcard was Sam Stockan. He is dressed in his finery to celebrate the occasion of Queen Victoria's Diamond Jubilee in 1897. The postcard itself was sent from Stromness to Glasgow in January 1905.

In 1872, when the Education Act made schooling compulsory for all children, Orkney was probably ahead of many other areas in having about 80% of its school-age children already enrolled at schools which were mainly run by church denominations. Until 1947 only a small minority of Orkney's pupils received a secondary education, attending either Kirkwall Grammar School or Stromness Academy. In that year, the school leaving age was raised to 15 and a wider provision of schooling was necessary.

109. "STROMNESS SCHOOL"
This anonymously-published postcard shows Stromness School as seen from the approach along Franklin Road. The school itself had an excellent view across the town's roofscape. A replacement primary school was built in the late-1960s and a new secondary school – Stromness Academy – was built on another site in the 1980s. The old school now houses the International Centre of Island Technology.

110. "THE BEACH, STROMNESS"
The beach on this postcard is near the Point of Ness, just to the south of Stromness. Across Hoy Sound is Hoy Low Lighthouse (on the north-western point of the island of Graemsay), with the hills of the island of Hoy in the background. What finer natural playground could any children hope for?

The parish of Birsay covers the north-western corner of the Mainland. It has a population of about 800, rather less than half the figure recorded when the population reached its peak in 1861. Birsay is generally an undulating, agricultural area, ending abruptly in the west at the magnificent bird-cliffs of Marwick Head. The quiet village of Birsay was once the centre of Norse power in Orkney.

Birsay *P.O. Orphir. 2:4103.*
Many thanks for lovely p.c.s recd today. Yes indeed Stonehaven is lovely. I've sent to Shetland for

111. "BIRSAY"
"This is the ruins of an old castle" wrote the postcard's sender (from Orphir post office) in February 1903. "You can also see the parish church and post office". The "castle" in this case is the Earl's Palace (the ruins of which can be seen on the right). The parish church (left) is St Magnus' Kirk, built in 1760 to replace an earlier church possibly built by the Norse Earl Thorfinn in about 1050.

EARL'S PALACE, BIRSAY, ORKNEY.

112. "EARL'S PALACE, BIRSAY"
Robert Stewart, the illegitimate son of King James V of Scotland, obtained the title and lands of the Earldom of Orkney in 1568 and, in about 1574, built in Birsay what in 1633 was described as "a sumptuous and stately dwelling". The Palace was built as a fortified residence. The great cliffs of Marwick Head can be seen in the background (right).

Towering cliffs can be found along various sections of Orkney's long coastline but none are more majestic than those rising up against the Atlantic on the islands' west coast. The huge bulk of Marwick Head, just south of the village of Birsay, has a special magnificence. Memories of the loss of *HMS Hampshire* during the First World War also give these particular cliffs a special poignancy.

113. "MARWICK HEAD AND KITCHENER MEMORIAL"
Marwick Head rises sharply from the Atlantic to a height of 283 feet. Its great bulk makes it look much higher. The cliff's eroded edges make excellent breeding sites for countless seabirds during the spring and summer months. On the highest point stands the square tower of the Kitchener Memorial. In the left background is the Brough of Birsay, a tidal island having important Pictish, Norse and early-Christian remains.

114. "MEMORIAL TO EARL KITCHENER, BIRSAY"
The 11,000 ton cruiser *HMS Hampshire*, with Field Marshall Earl Kitchener of Khartoum (Minister of War) on board, was on its way to Russia – reportedly to rally the failing armies of Czar Nicholas II – when it struck a German mine off Marwick Head on 5th June, 1916. Lord Kitchener and all but 12 of the ship's crew perished. The memorial tower at Marwick Head was funded by public subscription and built in 1924.

The parishes of Firth and Harray have a combined population of just over 1,000. Both parishes have rich agricultural farmland and, on the higher ground, extensive tracts of open moorland. The latter serves as an invaluable habitat for some of Orkney's rare birds. Finstown is the only settlement of any size in the parish of Firth.

115. "FINSTOWN"
Finstown is said to be named after an Irish soldier, called Phin, who retired here in about 1822 at the end of the Napoleonic wars. He established an ale-house, known as the "Toddy Hole", on the Kirkwall-Stromness road. Snugly located in a valley and at the head of the Bay of Firth, Finstown is today Orkney's third largest settlement.

116. "MANSE OF HARRAY"
"What do you think of this photo? It is my abode", wrote Mabel Dickey to Mrs Cunningham in Londonderry on 4th September, 1907. She posted the postcard in Finstown that day. Tom Kent's postcard shows St Michael's Manse, built in 1856 for the Reverend Samuel Traill.

Harray is the only Orkney parish without a coastline. Without access to the sea, the parish has long depended on its farming. As a consequence, its population of about 500 lives in small, scattered townships. The award-winning Corrigall Farm Museum, re-creating a nineteenth-century Orkney farmstead, is situated in the parish.

117. "THE CROSSROADS, DOUNBY"
Dounby is situated where the parishes of Birsay, Harray and Sandwick meet. Its location at an important crossroads in central Mainland led to the development of shops and facilities serving the local area. A post office first opened in Dounby in 1873. The Smithfield Hotel (shown on the next postcard) is situated at the crossroads (centre, right).

118. "SMITHFIELD HOTEL, DOUNBY"
Although this postcard has no publisher's name, it was probably produced as an advertising card for the Smithfield Hotel itself. The hotel is still instantly recognisable from this postcard.

The parish of Holm (pronounced "Ham") is the Mainland of Orkney's southernmost parish. Its village, St Mary's, faces St Mary's Bay, an eastern extension of Scapa Flow. From a point due east of St Mary's, the Churchill Barriers carry the road which links Mainland to the islands of Burray and South Ronaldsay.

119. "ST MARY'S, HOLM"

St Mary's grew as a result of the wealth earned from the herring fishing industry in the nineteenth century. The village straggles along the shore of St Mary's Bay and consists of single- and two-storey fishermen's cottages. The small boats in the foregound are typical Orkney "yoles" whilst the large, Kirkwall-registered fishing boat in the centre is the type of boat called a "Fifie".

120. "GRAEMESHALL, HOLM"

Graemeshall, to the east of St Mary's village, was the home of the Graham (later Graeme) family from 1626 to 1960. The present house was built in 1874, incorporating part of the seventeenth-century house and was extended in 1898. This postcard bears a "St Mary's Holm" postmark of 22nd June, 1909. "This view I am sending you", the message reads, "is the house where I am nursing ... The garden ... is quite a picture, one mass of bloom".

THE MAINLAND
SANDWICK

The parish of Sandwick is situated on the west coast of the Mainland and to the
north of Stromness. Its population of about 800 lives in scattered townships. The area
is known for its interesting coastal scenery, especially the great sweeping curve of the Bay
of Skaill and the cliffs and rock-stacks at Yesnaby. It is even better known as the location
of Skara Brae, one of the most fascinating archaeological sites in the British Isles.

121. "THE BAY OF SKAILL"
The Bay of Skaill is the point at which the Atlantic has made its greatest
incursion into the Mainland's west coast. William Hourston's postcard has
captured a view of the Bay's beautiful beach on a fine summer's day.

122. "PREHISTORIC VILLAGE OF SKARA"
Tom Kent's multi-view postcard shows a number of the features which make Skara
Brae such an interesting and important site. Together with Jarlshof in Shetland, it is one of
the best preserved prehistoric villages in Britain. Its state of preservation is so remarkable
that it does not take a great deal of effort to imagine the lives of its former inhabitants.

THE MAINLAND
SKARA BRAE, SANDWICK

Skara Brae is situated on the shores of the Bay of Skaill and consists of a series of rectangular, stone-built dwellinghouses, all connected by inter-connecting passages. Evidence suggests that the village was occupied for a period of about 600 years from 3,100 to 2,500 BC. This tightly-knit community of about 50 people would have been engaged in fishing, animal husbandry and cereal-growing.

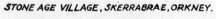

123. "STONE AGE VILLAGE, SKERRABRAE"
Each of Skara Brae's six dwellinghouses consists of a relatively spacious single room with thick, dry-stone walls, surviving in places to a height of nine feet. The quality of the workmanship involved in their construction is quite staggering. In the background of this view of the site stands Skaill House, one of Orkney's finest mansions.

124. "SKARA BRAE"
Tom Kent photographed the excavation of Skara Brae from 1927 onwards, recording the works undertaken. From the number of photographs taken it is reasonable to assume that Skara Brae was one of his favourite places. The building in this photograph is isolated from the remainder, leading to the conclusion that it served as a workshop rather than a dwelling.

THE MAINLAND
SKARA BRAE, SANDWICK

Skara Brae may well have been abandoned by its inhabitants because of a persistent threat from encroaching sand. The sand-dunes which eventually covered the site protected and preserved it until a severe storm in 1850 once more revealed what had remained hidden for over four thousand years. Examinations were made at different times before 1914 but the excavation and restoration we see today was largely the work of Professor V. Gordon Childe, acting for the Office of Works, from 1927.

125. "SKARA BRAE"
This anonymously-published postcard shows the remarkably high standard of the workmanship achieved by the builders over five thousand years ago. One of Skara Brae's custodians is shown giving a typically lively and informative interpretation of the features of building No. 1.

126. "CHAMBER No. 7, SKARA VILLAGE"
The interior of building No. 7 shows the remarkable state of Skara Brae's preservation. The stone slabs we see today were part of the original furnishings but we have to visualise the beds covered with animal skins or heather and the shelves bearing decorated pottery jars. The house would have been roofed with skins or turf, supported on rafters made of driftwood or whales' ribs.

THE MAINLAND
SANDWICK

The Mainland's west coast is noted for its cliffs and headlands, where battles against the Atlantic gales have been fought since time immemorial. The coastline shows ample battle scars and, because of this, is a place of great natural beauty.

127. "THE HOLE O' ROW, SANDWICK"

Hole o' Row is a striking natural chasm in the cliffs at Row Head, at a point where the Atlantic has pierced a large hole right through the cliff. Row Head itself forms the southern flank of the Bay of Skaill.

128. " 'YESNABY CASTLE' ROCK, SANDWICK"

"No-one should miss seeing the incredible rock scenery of Yesnaby, a tangled skein of rocks, cliffs and deep water, magnificent in its starkness", stated an earlier official guide-book. The Yesnaby Castle rock-stack, approximately half-way along Mainland's west coast, is often confused with the Old Man of Hoy. This postcard was posted at Melsetter (Hoy) in October 1908 and sent to Dingwall.

THE MAINLAND
STENNESS

With about 360 inhabitants, the parish of Stenness is one of the smallest of the Mainland parishes. It is noted primarily for the richness of its archaeological remains. The Standing Stones of Stenness, the Ring of Brodgar and the great tomb of Maeshowe are some of Europe's most important prehistoric sites.

Stenness Hotel and Loch, near Stromness.

129. "STENNESS HOTEL AND LOCH, NEAR STROMNESS"
The Stenness Hotel was subsequently renamed the Standing Stones Hotel in recognition of its close proximity to the great prehistoric monuments of the Stones of Stenness and the Ring of Brodgar. The hotel's advertisement in an old guide-book extolled the virtues of its "beautiful location on the shores of Loch Stenness on the main road between Kirkwall and Stromness" and its "first class cuisine" and "excellent loch fishing".

ALONG THE LOCH OF STENNESS. ORKNEY.   W. H.

130. " ALONG THE LOCH OF STENNESS"
William Hourston's superb photograph of the shores of the Loch of Stenness shows Orkney at its idyllic best. With the soft, rolling hills of West Mainland interspersed with well-stocked trout lochs, the area represents a veritable paradise for naturalists, ornithologists and fishermen alike.

Close to the point in the parish of Stenness where a narrow causeway (now carrying the B9055 road) separates the Loch of Harray from the Loch of Stenness, stands a remarkable and unrivalled collection of prehistoric sites. The reason for Orkney's neolithic settlers constructing the great tomb of Maeshowe and the stone circles of Stenness and Brodgar at this location are now lost in the mists of time.

131. "MAESHOWE"

Maeshowe, just to the north of the main Kirkwall-Stromness road, is probably the finest prehistoric tomb in Europe. It is thought to date from approximately 2750 BC and is an eloquent testament to the skills of Orkney's neolithic masons. The great mound rises to a height of 23 feet and encloses a magnificent main chamber and three small side chambers. It was excavated in 1861 when it was found that Norse raiders had entered the tomb about 700 years earlier and left a large number of runic inscriptions on the interior walls.

132. "CIRCLE OF STENNESS"

The Stones of Stenness are still an impressive sight, even though only four of the original twelve stones in the circle now survive. Analysis suggests that the circle dates from about 2500 BC. The circle was originally surrounded by a substantial ditch.

THE MAINLAND
STENNESS

The stone circles of the Ring of Brodgar and the Stones of Stenness, together
with the Maeshowe tomb and various isolated stones, must have constituted a great
ceremonial complex in the heart of Orkney. The construction of such monumental
works imply an organised and developed society in these northern islands.

133. "THE WATCH STONE"
The Watch Stone is a striking, solitary monolith, standing about 18 feet high, at the
edge of the narrow causeway separating the Loch of Stenness from the Loch of Harray.
Its location was probably connected in some way with the near-by Stones of Stenness
(postcard No. 132) but knowledge of its exact purpose has long since been loSt

Stones of Stenness, Orkney

134. "STONES OF STENNESS"
Despite its title, this postcard actually shows the impressive stone circle of the Ring of Brodgar.
There may originally have been as many as 60 standing stones forming a huge circle about 340 feet
in diameter, but only 27 still stand today. The Ring of Brodgar, with its surrounding ditch and outlying
burial mounds, dates from about 2500 BC and may have been designed as a lunar observatory.

Midsummer in Orkney is the time for dazzling displays of wild-flowers. In earlier years, blue lupins were part of this spectacle. The plants were native neither to Orkney nor to Britain in general and it is thought that they were introduced to Orkney in about 1860 by Lieutenant-General Frederick William Traill Burroughs, laird of the Westness estate on Rousay, who had served with the British army in India.

135. "THE PATH THROUGH THE WILD LUPINS"
Having originally been introduced to enrich the quality of the soils of Orkney's heathlands, cultivation of the lupins quickly spread. The striking blue haze of lupins became a familiar sight of an Orkney summer, particularly in the Mainland parishes of Harray and Sandwick.

136. "LUPIN TIME, LOCH OF STENNESS"
Methods of cultivation change as the decades pass and, sadly, modern farming has eradicated Orkney's lupins in all but the small, isolated patches where they naturalised and continue to flourish.

ORKNEY AT WAR

At the beginning of the twentieth century, Great Britain and Germany were engaged in a massive race to develop their military power. As tensions grew, the Admiralty began to take an interest in using Scapa Flow – the 'inland sea' bounded by Mainland Orkney and the islands of Hoy, Burray and South Ronaldsay – as a naval anchorage. Using Scapa Flow, it was hoped to contain the German fleet in the North Sea.

FIRST DIVISION CRUISERS AT SCAPA FLOW, ORKNEY. I.K.

137. "FIRST DIVISION CRUISERS AT SCAPA FLOW"
Before war broke out in 1914, the Royal Navy regularly held exercises in Scapa Flow. With war imminent, the British Home Fleet assembled in Scapa Flow in the summer of 1914. Its commander, Sir John Jellicoe, the First Sea Lord, was only too aware that the Flow's defences were not ideal but Winston Churchill, the First Lord of the Admiralty, took the necessary measures to block several of its entrance channels.

EVENING LIGHT OVER SCAPA FLOW, ORKNEY

138. "EVENING LIGHT OVER SCAPA FLOW"
This postcard might well be entitled "The calm before the storm". When news was received that the German Hochseeflotte (High Seas Fleet) had put to sea, nearly 150 British ships set out to face them. On 31st May, 1916, the British fleet faced 99 technically-superior German ships in the largest sea battle ever to have been fought. The Battle of Jutland led to the loss of 14 British and 11 German ships and about 8,000 men. The battle was essentially inconclusive but it ensured that the German fleet was never to venture out in force again.

Scapa Flow was to be the main base of the British Home Fleet during both World Wars. As many as 20,000 men were sometimes stationed at Scapa Flow. Many hated what could be a monotonous existence but many servicemen long remembered the genuine hospitality shown to them by the people of Orkney.

139. "LYNESS NAVAL BASE, HOY"
The chief naval base in Scapa Flow during the First World War had been at Longhope, South Walls, but in 1919 the base moved to Lyness, on the east coast of Hoy. The Lyness base was to grow beyond all recognition after 1919 as the Second World War loomed. The naval base was officially closed in March 1953 and now the Lyness Interpretation Centre houses a fascinating selection of items from two World Wars.

140. "SCAPA SEAPLANE STATION"
By 1916 the Royal Navy had established a seaplane station at Houton in the Mainland parish of Orphir. Seaplanes based here were used on submarine-hunting patrols. The action of German U-boats in laying mines and attacking shipping, meant that the seaplanes' role was an important one. In 1923 the local Health Board acquired part of the redundant buildings (those nearest the mast in this photograph) and, in the following year, opened the Scapa Tuberculosis Pavilion.

ORKNEY AT WAR
THE SCUTTLING OF THE GERMAN FLEET

On 21st November, 1918, the German Imperial Navy's mighty Hochseeflotte
formally surrendered to the Allied forces. This was shortly after the signing of
the Armistice which brought the First World War's protracted hostilities to an end.
The first of 74 German ships were to enter Scapa Flow under escort two days later.

141. "THE GERMAN FLEET AS SEEN FROM HOUTON SEAPLANE STATION"
Tom Kent's postcard gives a good impression of the spectacle afforded by the sight
of German warships at their place of internment in Scapa Flow. The Bay of Houton
was the location of a Royal Navy Air Station during the First World War and today
is the site of the terminal for ferry services from the Mainland to Hoy and Flotta.

142. "GERMAN WARSHIPS INTERNED IN SCAPA FLOW"
From the respective positions of the German ships in J. Omond's postcard it is possible to surmise
that the pictured ships are the *Cöln, Frankfurt, Bremse, Brummer* (all cruisers), *Grosser Kurfürst,
Bayern* (both battleships), *Emden* (the fleet's flagship) and *Friedrich der Grosse* (battleship).

ORKNEY AT WAR
THE SCUTTLING OF THE GERMAN FLEET

Throughout the winter of 1918/19 and for a period of almost seven long months,
the ships of the German Navy were interned in Scapa Flow. The fleet's skeletal crew
of 1,800 men were not permitted to visit neighbouring ships and were not to set foot
ashore for 230 days. Understandably, they were in a state of near-mutiny.

German Fleet in Scapa Flow as it appeared just before being scuttled by Admiral Von Reuter's orders.

(534)

Copyright. H.M.Scrivens, Photographer, Oban.

143. "GERMAN FLEET IN SCAPA FLOW AS IT APPEARED JUST BEFORE BEING SCUTTLED BY ADMIRAL VON REUTER'S ORDERS"

In June 1919, the terms of the Treaty of Versailles were made known. Germany's government
was given a deadline of 21st June to indicate its acceptance of what it viewed to be harsh conditions.
In Scapa Flow, Rear-Admiral Ludwig von Reuter, commander of the interned German fleet,
had made secret plans to scuttle his ships in the event of hostilities breaking out anew.

German Destroyers Sinking.

144. "GERMAN DESTROYERS SINKING"

Knowing that the German government was hesitating to sign the Treaty but not being aware
that the stipulated deadline for acceptance of its terms had been extended, von Reuter was
convinced that war would be resumed and that the British would seize his fleet. At noon on 21st
June he gave the order to scuttle the entire fleet to prevent the ships falling into British hands.

ORKNEY AT WAR
THE SCUTTLING OF THE GERMAN FLEET

Rear-Admiral Ludwig von Reuter's order to scuttle the entire German fleet was
carried out with great efficiency and took the British forces by complete surprise.

145. "BAYERN'S FINAL PLUNGE"
On 21st June, a party of children from Stromness
was on a school outing to see the German Navy.
Aboard the Flying Kestrel they were admiring the
warships of the Kaiser's fleet when von Reuter's order
was carried out and, suddenly, the ships began sinking
all around them. The battleship *Bayern*, the German
Navy's most powerful ship, began sinking by the stern.

146. "GERMAN SHIPS SINKING AT SCAPA FLOW"
Postcard publishers were quick to exploit what
they thought would be a huge interest in the event.
This anonymously-published postcard has no sender's
message but was obviously sent in an outer envelope
as the imprint of a machine cancellation dated
27th June, 1919 (just six days after the scuttle took
place) can easily be discerned on the reverse.

ORKNEY AT WAR
THE SCUTTLING OF THE GERMAN FLEET

As the greatest scuttling of all time was taking place, the British fleet was absent on exercises in the Atlantic. The few British sailors remaining at base in Scapa Flow tried to board the sinking German ships and to run them ashore. In general, however, little could be done to prevent 74 German warships plunging to the bottom of Scapa Flow.

147. "BRITISH BOARDING PARTY ALONGSIDE GERMAN DESTROYER 21.6.1919"
C. W. Burrows' photograph shows a detachment of Royal Marines from *HMS Resolution* endeavouring to board the German battleship *Grosser Kurfürst*. The latter ship had been built in Hamburg and launched in May 1913. She came to rest in waters to the north of the small island of Cava and was finally to be salvaged in April 1933.

148. "CREW OF A GERMAN DESTROYER TAKING TO THE BOATS 21.6.1919"
Amidst the confusion of the scuttle, shots were fired from the British ships in an attempt to prevent the total loss of all the German warships. Nine German sailors were killed during the day's events.

With the mighty German High Seas Fleet now at the bottom of Scapa Flow or beached on its shoreline, Rear-Admiral von Reuter was taken aboard *HMS Revenge* to face the anger of the British commander. Von Reuter stated that he was certain that, if the circumstances were reversed, the British commanding officer would have taken the same action.

149. " 'EMDEN' AGROUND AT SWANBISTER BAY 21.6.19"
The Light-Cruiser *Emden* had been built at Bremen and launched in February 1916. She was Rear-Admiral von Reuter's flagship from which, at 10.30am on 21st June, 1919, he gave the order to scuttle the entire fleet at noon. The *Emden* itself was grounded in Swanbister Bay (part of Scapa Flow). The ship was later to be given to France as part of war reparations. She was finally to be scrapped in 1926.

150. "BATTLE CRUISER 'HINDENBURG' "
Regarded as being the very latest in German naval technology, the 28,000 ton battle-cruiser *Hindenburg* had been built at Wilhelmshavn and launched with a great deal of ceremony in 1915. When scuttled on 21st June, 1919, the ship came to rest in eleven and a half fathoms of water. She was successfully salvaged in the early 1930s and was towed to Rosyth, Fife, for breaking up.

ORKNEY AT WAR
THE SCUTTLING OF THE GERMAN FLEET

The first serious attempts to salve the 74 scuttled German warships was made in 1924. The firm of Cox & Danks were eventually to raise two battleships, four battle-cruisers, one light-cruiser and 26 destroyers. Metal Industries continued the work in the 1930s and finally closed its Lyness depot in 1947. Eventually, the price of scrap metal could no longer pay the expense of the salvage operations and the salvage work was generally discontinued.

151. "SALVING GERMAN DESTROYER G102"
Torpedo-Destroyer G102 was part of the fleet's No.II Flotilla. The vessel had a 1,116 ton weight and a speed of 33½ knots and had been built at Kiel. This particular ship was recovered from the waters off the east coast of the small island of Rysa (north-east of Lyness).

152. "SALVAGE PARTY WORKING ON A GERMAN DESTROYER"
When large-scale salvage operations finally came to an end, three battleships and four light-cruisers still remained on Scapa Flow's seabed and remain there to this day. The wrecks' continued existence make Scapa Flow a diving centre of international importance.

ORKNEY AT WAR
WAR MEMORIALS

The Great War ended in 1918 and memories of the enormous losses sustained during the four long and bloody years occupied the nation's thoughts for many years thereafter. Towns and villages great and small erected memorials to commemorate the dead. Orkney, which had suffered heavy losses in proportion to its population, was no exception. War memorials were unveiled in virtually every community in the islands in the years after 1918.

153. "KIRKWALL AND ST OLA MEMORIAL – UNVEILED BY GENERAL LORD HORNE 17.10.23"

A vast crowd assembled in Broad Street, Kirkwall, on 17th October, 1923, for the official unveiling by General Lord Horne of the Kirkwall and St Ola war memorial. The dignified memorial was set into the boundary wall on the Cathedral's north-west side and flanked new entrance gates to the kirkyard.

154. "EDAY MEMORIAL UNVEILED 4.2.20"

Smaller but equally dignified war memorials were erected throughout Orkney. Each community suffered losses they could never afford from their small populations. This unveiling ceremony, photographed by Tom Kent, took place on the island of Eday on 4th August, 1920. The memorial itself was erected half way between the main communities at the north and south end of the island.

The eastern entrances to Scapa Flow had been blocked by blockships during the First World War but the effects of wind and currents had subsequently rendered the defences incomplete. After war had broken out in 1939 and before action could be taken to improve the defences, a German U-boat, *U-47*, passed through Kirk Sound and, at 1.00am on 14th October, 1939, torpedoed the *Royal Oak*. The British battleship sank within 15 minutes with a loss of 833 of the total crew of 1,200.

CHURCHILL BARRIER, ORKNEY.

155. "CHURCHILL BARRIER"
Winston Churchill, as First Lord of the Admiralty, ordered that Scapa Flow's eastern entrances must be closed. In response, about 66,000 five and ten ton concrete blocks were constructed and used to seal the approaches. From early 1942 onwards, most of the labourers were Italian prisoners of war. The greatest depth of water crossed by the barriers was about 55 feet. It was dangerous work and was to cost ten lives during the four-year construction period.

CHURCHILL BARRIERS, SCAPA FLOW, ORKNEY

156. "CHURCHILL BARRIERS, SCAPA FLOW"
The total length of the four Churchill Barriers is about one and a half miles. The total cost of construction is thought to have been about £2.5 million. A road was built along the top of the four barriers and was officially opened on 12th May, 1945. This created a road link between Mainland Orkney and the islands of Burray and South Ronaldsay via the small, uninhabited islands of Lamb Holm and Glims Holm.

THE SOUTH ISLES
THE ITALIAN CHAPEL

During the Second World War, the small island of Lamb Holm was the site of Prisoner of War Camp No. 60. This was the place of detention of about 550 Italian PoWs captured during the North Africa campaigns. They were brought to Orkney to supplement the civilian workforce employed on the construction of the four Churchill Barriers. The PoWs were given permission to use an army Nissen hut as a chapel. The end result of their labours between 1942 and 1944 was not only a testament to the PoWs' personal faith but has also left one of Orkney's most extraordinary buildings and one of its main tourist attractions.

157. "ITALIAN P.O.W. CHAPEL, LAMBHOLM, SCAPA FLOW"
Showing extraordinary craftsmanship and artistry and using whatever materials came to hand, the Italian PoWs disguised the front of the nissen hut with a decorated concrete facade. The concrete bases of other buildings in PoW Camp No. 60 can clearly be seen in this postcard.

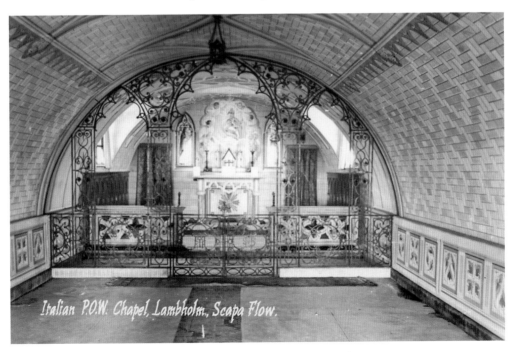

158. "ITALIAN P.O.W. CHAPEL, LAMBHOLM, SCAPA FLOW"
The vaulted interior of the decorated hut was lined with plasterboard and decorated to resemble brick- and stone-work. Over the altar, Domenico Chiocchetti painted the Madonna and Child, based on a picture he had carried with him throughout the war. From his home in Moena, in the Italian Dolomites, Chiocchetti returned to Orkney in 1960 to renovate the chapel's decorations. On his return visit he was afforded a full civic welcome, which was very different to the circumstances of his first visit!

THE SOUTH ISLES
ST. MARGARET'S HOPE, SOUTH RONALDSAY

St Margaret's Hope is the main settlement on the island of South Ronaldsay. There are several theories about the origins of the village's unusual name. One suggests that it was named after Margaret, the Maid of Norway and heir to the Scottish throne, who died in Orkney in 1290 on her way to marry the future Edward II of England. Other suggestions are that it was named after Margaret, the saintly Queen of Scotland (who died in 1093) or perhaps St Margaret of Antioch whose cult was popular for a time.

159. "ST MARGARET'S HOPE"
This "Kent's Viking Series" postcard shows a panoramic view of the village from the west. St Margaret's Hope developed as a herring-fishing station during the industry's boom years in the nineteenth century but was never as important as South Ronaldsay's neighbouring island of Burray.

GOING OUT TO MEET THE "ST. OLA" AT ST. MARGARET'S HOPE, ORKNEY

160. "GOING OUT TO MEET THE ST OLA AT ST MARGARET'S HOPE"
This postcard was "Specially printed for J. Spence & Son, St Margaret's Hope". It was sent from St Margaret's Hope to Northampton in about 1905 (the year on the postmark is unclear). Between 1892 and the Second World War, the Scrabster-Stromness ferry called at St Margaret's Hope. A small boat would sail out to meet the incoming ferry and exchange mail and passengers.

THE SOUTH ISLES
ST. MARGARET'S HOPE, SOUTH RONALDSAY

When the route of the Scrabster-Stromness ferry was changed at the end of the
Second World War and St Margaret's Hope was no longer a port of call, the relative
importance of the village began to decline. The importance of the village to South
Ronaldsay was further eroded when the Churchill Barriers were constructed. The islands
of Burray and South Ronaldsay today have a combined population of about 1,100.

161. "ST MARGARET'S HOPE – THE FRONT"
St Margaret's Hope village essentially consists of two main streets – Back Road
and Front Road. This Valentine's postcard shows part of Front Road. The three large
houses on the left, each presenting their gable-end to the street, are a group of substantial
eighteenth-century merchants' houses. The third of the three was the St Margaret's
Hotel at this time. Each had been built with stone piers projecting into the bay.

162. "ST MARGARET'S HOPE"
This postcard has no details of publisher or photographer but may possibly have been produced
by Tom Kent. It shows Front Road after a heavy snowfall. This photograph was taken just a short walk
from the place where the previous photograph was taken. St Margaret's Hotel is on the extreme left.

THE SOUTH ISLES
GRAEMSAY

The small island of Graemsay lies between Stromness and the island of Hoy. Its population reached a peak of 286 in 1851 but has fallen to about 40 today. The islanders have traditionally been employed in crofting and seafaring. Reflecting the island's important position in the western approaches to Scapa Flow and Stromness harbour, Graemsay boasts two lighthouses, Hoy High and Hoy Low, both built in 1851 to designs by Alan Stevenson.

INLAND
10.
STAMP.
FOREIGN
10.
PRINTED IN
BRITAIN.

163. "HOY HIGH LIGHTHOUSE, GRAEMSAY"
Hoy High lighthouse has aptly been described as "the Rolls Royce of Orkney's lighthouses". Its tower rises to a height of 103 feet at Graemsay's north-easternmost point. The tower's classical architecture is shown on this postcard dating from the early years of the twentieth century. The tall chimneys seen on the postcard project from the single-storey, flat-roofed keepers' houses.

164. "HOY HIGH LIGHTHOUSE"
William Hourston's postcard view of Hoy High lighthouse dates from the 1930s. It gives a good impression of the height of the elegant tower. The cloud-capped mountains of Hoy, about four miles to the south-west, can be seen in the background.

THE SOUTH ISLES
HOY

The name "Hoy" means "high island" and is derived from the Old Norse word "Ha-ey". It is a fitting name for Orkney's second largest island since the island is known for its mountainous landscape. The Ward Hill (1,570 feet), at Hoy's northern end, is Orkney's highest point. A spectacular rampart of cliffs line Hoy's west and north coasts, punctuated only by the dramatic sweep of Rackwick Bay.

165. "HOY MANSE"
Sir Walter Scott visited Hoy in 1814 and took tea at the local manse. The manse – now Burra House, situated near the shore on the Bay of Creekland and not far from Moness pier – features on this pre-1914 postcard produced by Tom Kent.

166. "ORGILL LODGE, HOY"
Orgil Lodge is situated in north Hoy, further up the road featured on the preceding postcard. The two postcards on this page were probably the result of the same visit made to Hoy by Tom Kent. This northern part of the island has suffered badly from the effects of depopulation. There were about 300 people living in Hoy's northern townships in the mid-nineteenth century, a number which had fallen to about 30 by 1970.

THE SOUTH ISLES
"THE HOY EXPRESS"

As a subject for Orcadian picture postcards in the Edwardian "golden age", "the Hoy Express" was almost as popular as the Old Man of Hoy or St Magnus' Cathedral. In the days before motorised transport, when horses and carts were still in regular use to carry the mail in rural Britain, Hoy's own mailcart – pulled by a bullock – was probably unique. Nicknamed "the Hoy Express", it was the only vehicle capable of traversing the rough moorland tracks which served as roads on Hoy at the time.

167. "THE HOY EXPRESS"

This postcard shows "the Hoy Express" outside Hoy post office. The island's first post office had been established at Linksness in 1879. The postcard was sent from Orgil Lodge to London and bears a splendid strike of the "HOY" postmark dated 10th August, 1909. This datestamp remained in use at the Hoy post office for almost 35 years after about 1900.

168. "THE HOY EXPRESS"

This later version of "the Hoy Express" postcard was published as part of "Leonards 'Orkney' Series". It is probable that the bullock-cart depicted was not the one used by the Post Office to convey the island's mails but, nevertheless, it makes a splendid subject for a postcard.

"The Hoy Express" was a service which came into existence in 1898 when a postal delivery service was established to link the Hoy post office (at Linksness) with the remote township of Rackwick. The two communities are on opposite sides of Hoy and were linked by a long, lonely track. "The Hoy Express" became an historic curiosity when Orkney's roads were upgraded and motorised transport came to the fore.

169. "THE HOY EXPRESS"
"A rustic pair!", the writer has written on the front of this early "Valentine's Series" postcard. It was sent from Kirkwall to Sale, Cheshire, in October 1903. The postcard shows the type of terrain across which "the Hoy Express" travelled. It seems to prove that this type of cart was perhaps the most appropriate vehicle for the task!

170. "FLOTTA EXPRESS"
Endeavouring to emulate the commercial success of "the Hoy Express" postcards of the Edwardian era, unknown publishers tried their hand at "the Flotta Express". It depicts the typical four-wheeled Orkney "sled" still in widespread use in Orkney's South Isles in the early years of the twentieth century. The island of Flotta lies to the east of Hoy.

THE SOUTH ISLES
RACKWICK, HOY

Rackwick, the only settlement on Hoy's west coast, is Orkney's most isolated community.
It is reached by a long, lonely road between Hoy's great hills. Rackwick was a typical
Orkney community, dependent on both crofting and fishing. Rural depopulation led to
an inevitable decline in the township's fortunes. At one time the population had dwindled
to just one and roofless crofthouses and untended fields were a melancholy sight.

171. "RACKWICK, HOY"
L. J. Smith of Stromness published this postcard with its fine panoramic view of
Rackwick. The community was obviously a thriving one when this photograph was
taken. In later years, just when it seemed that the whole township would be abandoned,
it began to take on a new lease of life. Rackwick's scenic splendours have led it to
become a holiday retreat and several of its abandoned crofts have been revitalised.

172. "RACKWICK, HOY"
Rackwick's curving beach is strewn with massive boulders, showing the enormous force exerted by
the sea on this exposed part of Orkney's coast. Despite this, the community existed in part on its fishing
skills. The decline of fishing in these hazardous waters echoed the decline of the community as a whole.

THE SOUTH ISLES
THE OLD MAN OF HOY

The Old Man of Hoy is perhaps the most famous sea-stack in the British Isles. It stands clear of the huge cliffs between St John's Head and Rora Head and rises to a height of 450 feet (the same height as St Paul's Cathedral). Created by the winds and waves of the mighty Atlantic, the Old Man of Hoy has defied the same forces from time immemorial.

173. "THE OLD MAN OF HOY"
The Old Man of Hoy has been a popular choice for postcards from the earliest days. The photograph from which this particular postcard was printed was taken by George Washington Wilson in the early 1890s, the postcard itself being published in the early years of the twentieth century.

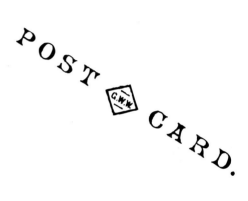

174. "THE OLD MAN OF HOY"
An excellent view of the Old Man of Hoy is often gained from the deck of the Scrabster-Stromness ferry. Weather permitting, the captain slows the ship and passengers gather along the starboard rail to view this natural spectacle. In the background of this "Kent's Series" postcard is the great bulk of St John's Head (1,140 feet).

Melsetter lies at the south end of Hoy and at the Head of North Bay. Melsetter House and its accompanying chapel and estate-workers' houses represents a remarkable series of buildings, rich in architectural interest. The house was requisitioned by the naval authorities during both World Wars. Today the house remains in private ownership.

175. "MELSETTER"
Having made his fortune from a leather business in Birmingham, Thomas Middlemore bought the large Melsetter estate for his retirement. In 1898 he employed William Lethaby to alter and furnish the old house. This proved to be an inspired choice since Lethaby was one of the leading figures in the Arts & Crafts movement. The house sits more comfortably in the Orkney landscape than do the baronial-style great houses elsewhere in Orkney.

176. "MELSETTER HOUSE AND CHAPEL"
Leading Arts & Crafts designers and manufacturers were chosen by Lethaby to furnish the house's interior. The small chapel of St Margaret and St Colm (centre right), built in the grounds of Melsetter House in 1900, was also designed by William Lethaby and contains stained-glass by Ford Maddox Brown and Edward Burne-Jones.

THE SOUTH ISLES
LONGHOPE, SOUTH WALLS

South Walls can be regarded as being a separate island in its own right since it was formerly
a tidal island, connected to neighbouring Hoy only by a narrow sandbank which could be crossed
at low tide. This neck of land – the Ayre – now carries the road linking the main communities
of Hoy and South Walls. The chief settlement of South Walls is the village of Longhope.

177. "VIEW AT LONGHOPE"
Longhope village straggles along the southern shore of the body of water also called
Longhope. This was formerly an important anchorage but, in later years, the focus of attention
for Scapa Flow's shipping moved away to Stromness and Lyness. Longhope has a famous lifeboat
station, situated near-by on the shore of Aith Hope. Having featured in many gallant rescues, the
lifeboat was itself the subject of tragedy in March 1969 when the entire crew of eight perished
in heavy seas whilst endeavouring to rescue the crew of a cargo ship in the Pentland Firth.

178. "LONGHOPE, ORKNEY, UNDER SNOW. VIEW FROM PIER"
Prominent in this unusual wintertime view of Longhope are the post office (centre left) and the Longhope
Hotel (centre, up the hill). Both buildings are featured on separate postcards on the next page.

LONGHOPE, SOUTH WALLS

Longhope Bay was an important naval anchorage during both World Wars. Although
Lyness was to become the chief naval base during the Second World War, it was at Longhope
that the chief military officer set up his headquarters during the First World War.

179. "LONGHOPE POST OFFICE AND PIER"
A post office opened in Longhope as long ago as 1832, emphasising the relative
importance of the village during the first half of the nineteenth century.

180. "LONGHOPE HOTEL"
During the First World War, the Longhope Hotel served as the headquarters of
the Admiral Commanding Orkney and Shetland. Both King George V and the Prince
of Wales (later King Edward VIII) stayed at the hotel whilst visiting the British fleet.

THE WRECK OF THE DINNINGTON, FEBRUARY 1906

Cantick Head lighthouse and the neighbouring uninhabited island of Switha featured in a dramatic
sea rescue on 16th February, 1906, when the 366 ton Sunderland-registered steamer *Dinnington*
– bound for Stornoway with a cargo of coal – encountered severe weather in the Pentland Firth.

CANTICK HEAD LIGHTHOUSE AND ISLAND OF SWITHA, ORKNEY.   Kent's "Viking" Series.

181. "CANTICK HEAD LIGHTHOUSE AND ISLAND OF SWITHA"

In pitch darkness and blinding snow, the *Dinnington* tried to run for cover at Longhope but ran
aground on rocks off Switha and started to break-up almost immediately. Two men were washed
overboard and drowned but the captain and the eight other crew members scrambled ashore at Switha.

THE SOUTH WALLS BOAT'S CREW WHO GALLANTLY RESCUED THE SURVIVORS OF THE CREW
OF THE S.S. DINNINGTON WRECKED AT SWITHA ORKNEY FEB 16th 1906 (J.OMOND).

182. "THE SOUTH WALLS BOAT'S CREW WHO GALLANTLY RESCUED THE SURVIVORS OF THE CREW OF THE S.S. DINNINGTON, WRECKED AT SWITHA. FEB 16th 1906"

The nine survivors from the wreck of the *Dinnington* were rescued in truly heroic
manner by six fishermen from South Walls who, having seen the ship's lights, set off
in atrocious conditions to find out what had happened to the ship and its crew. Following
the rescue, the six boatmen, William and Bremner Taylor, William Groat, Edward Jameson,
W. Chiene and D. Fiddler (all pictured) were each awarded the RNLI's Silver Medal.

THE NORTH ISLES
ROUSAY

Rousay is separated from the west Mainland by the narrow strait of Eynhallow Sound. Like Hoy, Rousay is mountainous, rising to a height of 821 feet at Blotchnie Fiold. The island has justifiably been called "the Egypt of the North", with its wealth of fascinating prehistoric monuments. These sites make Rousay a place of national historic importance.

183. "EARLY MORNING AT THE PIER, ROUSAY"
The pier at Trumland is the landing place for the ferry service linking Rousay with Tingwall on Orkney's Mainland. Trumland village itself is the main centre for the island's scattered population which now numbers about 200. The land can be seen rising steeply behind the village to reach the summit at Blochnie Fiold, now included in an RSPB reserve.

Inland
½ d.
Stamp
Foreign
1 d.
Printed in Saxony

184. "TRUMLAND HOUSE, ROUSAY"
Built for Lieutenant-General Frederick William Traill Burroughs in 1872/3, Trumland House was designed by the same architect as Balfour Castle on Shapinsay (postcard No. 190). The huge cost of the house was partly responsible for Burroughs' debts which, in turn, led him to become a notorious landlord, systematically persecuting his tenants by rack-renting and evictions. A serious fire damaged much of the fine interior in 1985.

Rousay's interior is predominantly mountainous and so the island's one main road runs in a roughly circular manner, generally following the coastline. To the east are views of the small, low-lying island of Egilsay, separated from its larger neighbour by Rousay Sound. Egilsay's population has fallen from 225 in 1831 to less than 50 today.

185. "SCABRA HEAD, ROUSAY"
At Rousay's westernmost point is Scabra Head, the start of an imposing series of cliffs whose banded and eroded strata provide an ideal breeding site for many varieties of seabird. Scabra Head is close to the sites of the great Midhowe Chambered Cairn (dating from about 3,500 BC) and the Midhowe Broch (dating from about 200 BC to 200 AD).

Orkney Herald Real Photo Series

186. "ST MAGNUS KIRK, EGILSAY. ROUND-TOWERED 12th CENTURY CHURCH"
The Norse Sagas tell us that rival cousins and joint Earls of Orkney, Hakon Paulsson and Magnus Erlandson, met at Egilsay in 1117, ostensibly to discuss their differences. Magnus was slain on Hakon's order. St Magnus Kirk was built on Egilsay in about 1136 to mark the site of the saint's martyrdom. The church remained in use until the mid-nineteenth century. The church's massive cylindrical tower is the only surviving example in Orkney and Shetland.

Shapinsay is separated from the nearest point of the Mainland by a narrow strait called
The String. The island's population today numbers about 320. The most noticeable feature
of this low-lying, green and fertile island is the straight roads and regular grid-iron field
patterns. The land was divided in this way by the nineteenth-century laird, David Balfour.

187. "BALFOUR VILLAGE"

Balfour village was originally called Shoreside and was developed in the late eighteenth
century to provide homes for the workers employed on the Balfour family's estate. David
Balfour renamed the village in the mid-nineteenth century to reflect the family's name.

188. "ELWICK, SHAPINSAY"

This panoramic view looks westwards across Elwick, the bay sheltered by the small, uninhabited
island of Helliar Holm. Balfour Castle (rear left) stands proudly amidst its plantation of trees.
The northern part of the village of Balfour can be seen between the castle and the shoreline.

THE NORTH ISLES
BALFOUR CASTLE, SHAPINSAY

In the south-east corner of Shapinsay lies Balfour Castle, built in the late 1840s for the local laird, David Balfour. Balfour had inherited a large family fortune, made in India, and he chose to display his wealth by building an imposing residence. His grandfather, Thomas, had bought the estate in 1782 and had arranged for the house of Cliffdale to be built. David Balfour engaged the Edinburgh architect David Bryce to enlarge Cliffdale in the then fashionable Baronial style.

189. "GATEHOUSE, BALFOUR CASTLE, SHAPINSAY"
Balfour Castle's gatehouse was built near the island's main pier in 1851. Intended to be a suitably imposing entrance to Balfour's newly-enlarged residence, the gatehouse served as a porter's lodge. In more recent years, it has been converted for use as a public bar.

Balfour Castle, Shapinsay, Orkney.

190. "BALFOUR CASTLE, SHAPINSAY"
This postcard shows the full glories (or excesses, depending on individual points of view) of the residence designed by Bryce for David Balfour. The castle is an outpouring of the Baronial style's love of square and conical towers, turrets and crow-stepped gables. The last member of Shapinsay's Balfour family died in 1961 and the castle was acquired by the Zawadski family under whose ownership the castle has been opened to the public.

THE NORTH ISLES
SANDAY AND STRONSAY

Sanday and Stronsay lie to the north-east of the Mainland of Orkney. Both islands have irregular coastlines with numerous peninsulas, headlands, bays and, particularly in the case of Sanday, great sweeping sandy beaches. Sanday has seen its population fall from 2,000 in 1881 to about 600 today whilst Stronsay's population has fallen from 1,200 to about 400 in the same period. Both islands have been served by Loganair's regular inter-island air services since 1967.

Kettletoft Pier, Sanday, Orkney.

191. "KETTLETOFT PIER, SANDAY"
Kettletoft was formerly the landing place on Sanday of the regular ferry service from Kirkwall. A ro-ro service now docks at Loth, on the island's south-western tip. The substantial stone-built complex of buildings at Kettletoft's pierhead were originally built for the fishing trade. Sanday's first post office opened here in 1839. Two regular Postbus services now link Sanday post office with all other parts of the island.

192. "WHITEHALL VILLAGE, STRONSAY"
Largely planned and built by Malcolm Laing of Kirkwall in the early nineteenth century, Whitehall – Stronsay's main settlement – grew to be one of Scotland's major herring fishing ports. Just before the First World War the village gave seasonal employment to about 2,400 fishermen and 1,500 support workers. By 1937 the industry had come to an end. This postcard was sent from Whitehall to Edinburgh in June 1928.

Taking all the islands together, Orkney has an enormously long coastline. Couple this with the storms which afflict the islands and the dangerous and complex tidal streams which hinder the movement of shipping, and it should come as no surprise to find that the islands have a long and tragic history of shipwrecks. Several of the wrecks which occurred during the early twentieth century were immortalised on picture postcards.

THE EDENMORE WRECKED AT PAPA-STRONSAY. ORKNEY. OCT 7TH 1909   NO.4.

193. "THE 'EDENMORE' WRECKED AT PAPA STRONSAY. OCT 7th 1909"
The 1,642 ton, Greenock-registered, three-masted cargo ship *Edenmore* was four days out from Hamburg, bound for Sydney, when she was driven onto rocks at The Roan, Papa Stronsay's easternmost point, during a severe storm on the night of Thursday, 7th October, 1909. She was the largest sailing ship ever to be wrecked in Orkney. All 25 members of the crew were rescued by Stronsay's lifeboatmen and taken to Whitehall. This postcard was sent from Kirkwall to Buckie a short while later, on 23rd October 1909. "… Lots of pianos on board", the writer states. "They are busy salving it but the vessel is becoming broken up".

194. "BURGH HEAD, STRONSAY, AND WRECK OF ST ROGNVALD"
The 1,053 ton *St Rognvald* was wrecked in dense fog on Burgh Head, Stronsay, on 24th April 1900 whilst on passage from Lerwick to Kirkwall. All 70 passengers were landed safely on Stronsay but the ship itself sank in deep water just over a week later. The ship had been built in 1883 and became the flagship of the North Company's fleet.

Westray lies about 24 miles north of Kirkwall and is served by regular ferry and air services. Although the island's population has fallen from 2,200 in 1881 to today's 700, the population loss has now been halted. Westray has gained a reputation for being the most prosperous of Orkney's North Isles, deriving its livelihood from its farmlands and its fishing fleet.

Inland Postage
½d.
Foreign Postage
1d

195. "S.S. ORCADIA"
R. H. Robertson of Westray published this postcard showing the *Orcadia*, the ship which provided the regular link between Kirkwall and Westray for 64 years. The *Orcadia* was first introduced in 1867 and was the second ship of that name to provide the service to the North Isles.

196. "PIEROWALL VILLAGE, WESTRAY"
Pierowall is Westray's main settlement. The village faces eastwards and is located towards the northern end of the island. Pierowall has long been an important harbour and is the main base for the island's modern fishing fleet. It was formerly the main port of call for the regular ferry sailings to Westray but the island is now served by a ro-ro ferry docking at Rapness, at Westray's southern end.

THE NORTH ISLES
WESTRAY

Westray, along with Sanday, is the largest of Orkney's North Isles and is also the most varied in its scenery. The island rises steeply to the west and reaches 555 feet at Fitty Hill. Westray's cliffs stretch for almost five miles and end dramatically at the island's north-westernmost point, Noup Head, now part of an important RSPB reserve.

PIEROWALL SCHOOL, WESTRAY, ORKNEY.

197. "PIEROWALL SCHOOL, WESTRAY"

"This is the school I taught in", wrote Betty Tulloch, posting this postcard at Westray post office (in Pierowall) on 16th September 1929. The postcard itself was published by R. H. Robertson of Westray and shows the village's substantial school buildings, set back a short distance from the bay.

NOUP HEAD LIGHTHOUSE, WESTRAY, ORKNEY.

198. "NOUP HEAD LIGHTHOUSE, WESTRAY"

The prominent white-painted tower of Noup Head lighthouse was built in 1898 to a design by David Stevenson. It was built to warn shipping off the North Shoal, a dangerous reef off Orkney's north-west coast. The lighthouse was made automatic in 1964. It shares its dramatic and lonely location with countless seabirds. The RSPB's Noup Head reserve is one of Orkney's – and Britain's – most important seabird colonies.

THE NORTH ISLES
WESTRAY AND PAPA WESTRAY

Westray and its smaller neighbour, Papa Westray, are separated by the narrow strait of
Papa Sound. Linking the two islands, however, is a scheduled flight by Loganair which, since
1974, has featured in the Guinness Book of Records as the world's shortest scheduled flight.
Loganair began its service to Westray and Papa Westray in 1967 and began to carry mail on the
flights three years later. The flight linking Westray and Papa Westray takes a mere 70 seconds.

Notland-Castle, Westray, Orkney. KENT'S SERIES

199. "NOTLAND CASTLE, WESTRAY"
Noltland Castle, overlooking Pierowall, was built in the mid-sixteenth century to serve Gilbert
Balfour, an adventurer in the court of Mary, Queen of Scots. It is obvious even today that Noltland
Castle, variously described as "strange and forbidding" and a "grim fortress", was built for defensive
purposes in troubled times. It is a Z-plan castle with thick walls pierced by numerous gun-loops.

KENT'S ORKNEY SERIES.

POST OFFICE, PAPA WESTRAY.

200. "POST OFFICE, PAPA WESTRAY"
A post office first opened on Papa Westray in 1879 when the island's population stood at about 380.
When, a century later, the population of Papey (as the island is usually known) had fallen below 100 and
the island was to lose its only shop, a co-operative was formed to halt the spectre of depopulation.
Happily, Papey's post office remains today in the same building at Backaskaill (on the island's west coast)
photographed for this "Kent's Orkney Series" postcard early in the twentieth century.

ACKNOWLEDGEMENTS

The following is a list of the photographers or publishers whose postcards
are featured in this book. The numbers are those identifying each of the 200
postcards reproduced in the volume. Where no reference number is given,
the photographer or publisher of a particular card is not known.

BAMFORTH & Co. Ltd., Holmfirth – 7
BURROWS, C. W., – 147, 148, 151, 152
CLOUSTON, R. W., Stromness – 95, 98
DAVIDSON'S Real Photographic Series – 1
D. R. G. B. – 101
EDWARDS, A. R. & Son, Selkirk – 4
"GROAT'S" Series – 176, 179
HOURSTON, William, Stromness – 3, 73, 86-88,
    91, 121, 130, 164
"JA-JA" – 83
KENT, Tom, Kirkwall – 5, 6, 10, 12, 13, 15, 17, 20,
    21, 24, 25, 27, 29, 31-34, 38, 40, 41, 49-51,
    53-55, 57, 58, 60, 61, 63, 65-68, 71, 74, 75, 77,
    81, 82, 89, 115, 116, 119, 122, 124, 126, 127,
    137, 140, 141, 149, 153, 154, 159, 165, 166,
    174, 177, 181, 184, 194, 199, 200
LEONARDS, The, Kirkwall – 16, 19, 30, 72, 76,
    78, 112, 113, 120, 134, 135, 168, 175, 185,
    189, 196

OMOND, J. – 52, 56, 59, 142, 182
ORKNEY HERALD, The, Kirkwall – 183, 186
RAE, John, Stromness – 2, 90, 92, 94, 104
ROBERTSON, E. H., Stromness – 129
ROBERTSON, R. H., Westray – 195, 197
SCHOLASTIC SOUVENIR Co., Blackpool – 123,
    139, 178
SCRIVENS, H. M., Oban – 143
SMITH, L. J., Stromness – 96, 100, 131, 171
SPENCE, David, Kirkwall – 42, 191
SPENCE, J. & Son, St Margaret's Hope – 160
S. P. T. & P. P. C. Co., Glasgow – 26
STEPHENSON, J. M., Kirkwall – 85
TUCK, Raphael & Sons, London – 45
VALENTINE & Sons Limited, Dundee – 11, 28,
    36, 43, 62, 84, 93, 99, 103, 111, 161, 169, 180
WILSON, George Washington, Aberdeen – 69,
    80, 105, 128, 173
W. R. S. Reliable Series 9, 23, 102, 106, 107, 167

BIBLIOGRAPHY

BURGHER, Leslie – *Orkney: An Illustrated
    Architectural Guide* (1991)
FERGUSON, David M. – *Shipwrecks of Orkney,
    Shetland and Pentland Firth* (1988)
LINKLATER, Eric – *Orkney and Shetland* (1965)
MacKAY, James A. – *Islands Postal History Series
    No. 7: Orkney & Stroma* (1979)
MOONEY, Harald L. – *St Magnus Cathedral*
    (Guidebook) (1985)
P.O.W. CHAPEL PRESERVATION COMMITTEE –
    Orkney's Italian Chapel (Guidebook) (1992)
ROYAL COMMISSION ON THE ANCIENT AND
    HISTORICAL MONUMENTS OF SCOTLAND,
    The – *Exploring Scotland's Heritage: Orkney
    and Shetland* (1985)

SCHEI, Liv Kjörsvik – *The Orkney Story* (1985)
SHEARER, John – *The New Orkney Book* (1966)
SIMMATH PRESS LIMITED, The – *Official Guide
    to the Orkney Islands* (1940s)
TAIT, Charles – *The Orkney Guide Book* (1991)
THOMPSON, William P. L. – *History of Orkney*
    (1987)
TINCH, David M. N. – *Shoal and Sheaf: Orkney's
    Pictorial Heritage* (1988)
VAN DER VAT, Dan – *The Grand Scuttle* (1982)
WRIGHT, Gordon – *Orkney from Old
    Photographs* (1981)

FAREWELL TO ORKNEY.   Kent's "Viking" Series.